Table of Contents

Introduction

■ ■

Congratulations.

You've just bought a book that will tell you all you need to know about DOS. Unlike other 'fat' DOS books, this one will NOT blind you with lots of technical information that only confuses. Also, it does not try to humour you with jokes. It concentrates on providing the real information; and teaches you all the essentials of DOS in a simple, concise style.

About this book

DOS *for beginners* has been designed to save you time. It is laid out in the form of a reference book, so that you can pick it up and read only what is necessary at the time. You don't even need to remember everything, just keep this book near your PC for easy access - when you need to look up something.

It is divided into four broad sections, each containing several chapters. There are 18 chapters in total plus a glossary of common computer and DOS terms.

How this book is organised

Each chapter, before it starts, summarises the topics that the chapter covers. These are the points under the "In this chapter you will learn...." line. So you can quickly decide whether you want to read the chapter now or leave it for later. Also, each section starts with a description outlining the contents of all the chapters within it.

When the screen contents are shown in the book and when you need to actually type something, the wording is shown in this typeface:

```
C> type here
```

When you need to press a combination of keys to perform a certain function, these keys are represented with a '+' in between. For example,

Alt+F

The above implies that you should press and hold down the Alt key, then tap the 'F' key once.

Finally, at various parts of this book, icons are used to help you learn DOS effectively. These are:

 This icon indicates something that you should try not to forget.

 Alerts you to potential problems, and usually implies that something must not be done, or at least some thought should be given to it first.

 These are tips which make computing more interesting and easier to use.

Essential Basics

If you don't have a clue about your computer, this section is for you. It explains the basic components of your machine and even how to switch it on. You'll discover exactly what DOS is and what it can do. Also covered are basic DOS commands, where to issue them and the easiest ways of working with them. You'll learn how to perform basic file operations like copy, delete, move and rename by typing commands and also by using the graphical shell.

Your Computer
and DOS

In this chapter you will learn ....

> About the basic components of your computer

> What exactly DOS is and what it can do for you

> How to switch on your computer

> About the events that occur automatically after you power-up

> How to exit from the DOS Shell/Windows if thrown into it

> What the DOS command prompt and command line are

> How to reset and turn off your computer

A computer system consists of hardware and software. Neither can function without the other. Software consists of instructions specially written to enable your computer to perform a useful task, like calculate the net pay or print a letter you have written on your computer. Hardware refers to the physical elements of your computer system.

These are the things you can see, feel and touch. They include components like the keyboard and the monitor. The keyboard is the main way of 'talking' to your computer. Whereas the monitor, or the screen as it is often called, is the main device for the computer to output information or to 'talk-back' to you. The other popular device used to output information is the printer of course, used to produce a hard copy.

Other hardware 'bits' include the system unit and the mouse. The mouse is increasingly used as an alternative to using a keyboard for input and selection of information. The system unit houses other important hardware components. Some of these you cannot see until you un-screw the casing - like the main mico-processor unit, memory chips and the hard disk drive. The floppy disk drive, however, is visible at the front of the system unit. Let us now look at these different hardware components in turn.

Micro-processor

The micro-processor is the 'brain' of the computer. It obeys and processes instructions given to it by programs (or software). It is the processor that performs all functions required of a computer system. A micro-processor is also sometimes referred to as the CPU *(Central Processing Unit)* or simply as a number, like 80386 or 80486. This number is a measure of the power of the micro-processor chip. The higher the number the more powerful the chip and therefore the more powerful the PC (Personal Computer).

Hence, you will notice that many product names for PCs include the chip number to indicate how fast or powerful the machine is going to be.

There are lots of chips inside the computer. They are black rectangular-shaped objects mounted on green circuit boards if you were to look inside by un-screwing the lid off the system unit. A chip is basically thousands of transistors concentrated in a small area. Each chip is programmed for a specific purpose. The largest one is usually the main micro-processor chip that controls everything; then there are specific chips controlling functions like your keyboard input and display. Even memory in your computer is available from a series of memory chips.

Memory

Memory (the most common type is called RAM - *Random Access Memory*) is a temporary storage medium, in the form of chips, inside the computer to store programs and data. It is used to store information you are working on at the time. Once you switch off the PC, the contents of the RAM is wiped off completely.

The other type of memory is called ROM - *Read Only Memory*. You cannot write here and its contents never gets wiped off. You do not need to worry about ROM at all.

The size of your RAM is quite important. You must have enough RAM to hold your software and data. If you are going to work with complex graphics, sound or animation, you'll need enough RAM to be able to store these large files.

Although the micro-processor will store a tiny bit of the program and data it is working on, it accesses RAM on a regular basis to refresh its own small storage.

Each memory (RAM) location can be regarded as a pigeonhole. One pigeonhole can only store one character, or a *byte* of information to use the correct computer term. This is the smallest unit of memory that can be transferred or processed. A thousand-byte (1,024 bytes to be precise) chunk of memory is termed a Kilobyte or Kb. A million bytes (1,048,576 bytes) of memory is called a Megabyte or Mb, and a huge billion bytes of memory (1,073,741,824 precisely) is actually a Gigabyte or Gb for short.

A byte is actually 8 bits. A *bit* is short for Binary digIT and it is either a '1' or a '0'. At the lowest level inside the computer, everything, including information you type and commands you give to the computer, is represented by a series of ones and zeros.

Disks and disk drives

Since RAM loses everything stored inside it when you switch off your computer, you need a more permanent storage medium. The most common type is offered by hard disks and floppy disks. A *disk drive* is used to read and write data stored on *disks*.

A disk can be thought of as a filing cabinet, allowing you to store several documents or files. A document, like a letter, report or even a memo is a basic unit of information. A group of related files, like all letters to your Bank Manager, will be kept in the same filing drawer. This in computer terms is a *directory*, containing files. This directory may be called BANKLTRS. You can have a directory within another directory (*sub-directory*) to logically organise all your files. Just in the same way as you would divide your filing drawer into sections. So for example, your BANKLTRS may be within a directory called FINANCE.

Disk drives and different types of disks are described in detail, later on in this book.

Keyboard

Apart from the main typewriter keys, your computer keyboard provides additional keys offering the following functions:

Enter. After you have typed a command from your keyboard press this key to send it to the computer. It is also used as a 'carriage return' on a typewriter to mark the end of a paragraph.

Ctrl and **Alt**. These stand for Control or Alternative keys respectively. They are usually used with other keys to perform functions controlled by software.

Function Keys. These are usually found along the top of the keyboard, labelled F1 to F12. They are again programmed to perform certain tasks depending on the software you are using. F1, for example will usually provide help in using the system.

Esc. Short for Escape, this key is usually used to cancel or back-out from a screen or option you have chosen. It is located at the top left-hand side of the keyboard.

Arrow Keys. There are four keys near the right side of the keyboard used to move the cursor to the left, right, up or down. A cursor is just a pointer displayed on the screen, telling you where the next bit of text you type will appear.

Shift and **Caps Lock**. If the Caps Lock light on your keyboard is lit, whatever you type will appear in capital letters unless you keep the Shift key depressed at the same time. If the Caps Lock light is not lit, then your main typewriter keys will appear in lower-case and if you want some of them to appear in capitals, just press the Shift key too for those letters. Press the Caps Lock key to turn on/off the Caps Lock light.

Num Lock and the **Numeric Keypad**. Like the **Caps Lock** key, the **Num Lock** key can be pressed to either enable you to use the numeric keypad found on most keyboards, or to turn this feature off. The latter will enable the keys to behave as cursor control keys (this includes the arrow keys already discussed as well as Page Up, Page Down, Home and End).

These are especially useful when using a word processor. For example, to move the cursor a whole page above or below the current position or to move the cursor at the start of the line (Home key) or at the end of the current line (End key).

If Num Lock is set on, (you'll always know this because the Num Lock light will be lit) then the numeric keypad behaves like a calculator allowing you to enter numeric data quickly. This is ideal when using a spreadsheet package for example. There are even keys representing numeric operations like / for division, * for multiplication, - for subtraction and + for addition.

Slash Keys. There are two types of slash keys on a PC keyboard:

Forward-slash: usually known just as the slash key, it leans from right to left. It is used as a symbol to represent division as already discussed and also as a separator for DOS switches. We will look at what a DOS switch is a little later when covering the DOS command structure, but for now it is an optional facility to tailor a DOS command. e.g. DIR /W. The slash key also represents a separator we can use in our own work or information we create (e.g. 12/02/94).

Backward-slash: commonly called the backslash, it leans in the opposite direction and is very important to DOS. More specifically, it represents the root directory in DOS and also acts as a separator between various directory names in a DOS path. You will learn about DOS directories, including the root and what a path is in Chapter 8.

Tab, **Backspace**, **Insert** and **Delete Keys**. These are mainly used in a word processor. The Tab key allows the cursor to jump a few pre-determined spaces so that you can align text easily and quickly under several columns. If you keep the Shift key depressed and then press the Tab key you'll usually obtain a backword-Tab.

The Backspace key deletes any text (including your DOS command), a character at a time from the left of the cursor. Whereas the Delete key (Del) deletes text from the right of the cursor. The Insert key (Ins), if selected, will insert text in between other text. If you press the Ins key again, you'll activate the over-write mode which effectively replaces or over-writes text that is already there with new text you type.

Mouse

A mouse is a pointing device used to communicate with your computer. It is particularly useful if you intend to use the DOS shell (see Chapter 5).

A mouse simply connects to the serial port at the back of your computer. It usually has two buttons you can press. However, you can buy a mouse with three buttons and program each one for a specific function. You can even buy a cordless mouse and there are other variations too!

To use it, first place it on a flat surface or use a mouse-mat. You will notice a cursor-block or a pointer moving on your screen as you move the mouse - which incidently has a small roller-ball at the bottom to allow it to move in any direction.

To make a selection, move the mouse pointer on top of an item and then press and release (or click) the left mouse button. Sometimes you can click twice in rapid succession to select an item (double-click).

A mouse can also be used to move items on the screen. This is achieved by first moving the mouse pointer over an item. Then, press and hold down the left mouse button and move the mouse to position the item. Finally, once you see the item in the new location, release the mouse button. This technique is called dragging the mouse.

What is DOS?

DOS is the most important software for the IBM personal computer (PC) or compatibles. It stands for Disk Operating System. Like any other computer operating system, DOS controls all activities on your computer. It decides where in memory to load your programs, transfers files from the hard disk to memory, accepts data from the keyboard, displays information on the screen, handles printing and so on.

We often take DOS for granted because we cannot see exactly what it is doing. Most of the time its activities are transparent to us. For example, when you are using a word processor on your PC and you decide to print a letter, your word processor program has to ask DOS for help (technical jargon is *makes a system call*). Now, it is easy to be fooled into thinking that the word processor program is communicating directly with the printer, but in fact it is DOS.

DOS also allows you to interact with it directly. It will accept instructions from you (the operator) and act on them. You can think of DOS as your personal attendant. By learning DOS, you'll be able to organise and manage the information in your computer and use it more easily. We will be looking at most of these features in this book. DOS also provides utilities, like the editor, which are software products in their own right.

Types of DOS

Although we use the term DOS, strictly speaking there are two main types, called: MS-DOS and PC-DOS. They are both developed by Microsoft corporation.

PC-DOS was developed specifically for the IBM PC. Microsoft still owns PC-DOS and earns large amounts of royalty fees from IBM. MS-DOS is very similar to PC-DOS, but Microsoft sells it to IBM clone manufacturers. It also now sells MS-DOS directly to customers as a shrink-wrapped software package like any other.

Both MS and PC DOS had to be very similar so that all the millions of IBM clones could have compatibility with the IBM PCs. By compatibility we mean that any software that works on an IBM PC should work in exactly the same manner on an IBM-compatible PC. Also peripherals like the printer, must be interchangeable between IBM and IBM-compatible PCs.

Switching "ON" your computer

Now that we understand some basic background, lets get down to some operational issues. And the first operation we all have to perform before we can do any work on our computer is of course to switch it on.

The ON/OFF switch may be at the front, side or the back of the system unit. Quite often ON is represented by a '1' and OFF by '0', probably because the computer works in the binary ones and zeros internally as already discussed. Anyway, you'll usually see a little power light come ON when the computer is switched ON just to confirm that it is ON.

What happens when you switch on your computer?

When you switch ON your computer, you will hear the noise of the internal cooling fan, taking air from the front of the machine and pushing it back. Ensure that your computer has enough room at the back for this ventilation. It should not be pressed right against the wall.

Then, you may see a flash of text displayed on the top right-hand side of the screen. This is usually a copyright message or a name of a branded product already installed, with its version number.

For the next few seconds, your computer will appear not to be doing anything. During this time it is checking all its internal parts, including the memory. The memory-test part is important - you may see on your screen, a series of numeric digits rapidly increasing in value as this test is being performed. Usually, these self-tests should not report errors. If you should however, at any time encounter an error, make a note of the error code and message and contact your supplier immediately.

Next, your PC will try to find DOS. It checks disk drive A first - you may notice the light for drive A come ON momentarily. Although nowadays most of us have DOS installed on disk drive C (or the hard disk), early PCs did not have a hard disk and DOS had to be loaded from drive A. For this historic reason and to be upward compatible, drive A is still searched first. If DOS is not found here, then disk drive C will be accessed and searched. If DOS is not found here either, then you will get a message to that effect and you will be required to insert the DOS disk (also referred to as the *system disk*) before continuing.

Assuming DOS is found, it is loaded automatically into memory. In this respect, DOS is a software product like any other application software products, including Lotus 1-2-3, Word, Excel or WordPerfect. The whole process described above, leading up to loading DOS is often referred to as *booting up*.

You can force this same chain of events by pressing Ctrl+Alt+Del keys together or pressing the RESET button found on many personal computers. Be careful though, because when you boot-up, everything in memory (or RAM to be precise) will be lost.

Once DOS is loaded, you will either see the graphical DOS shell, the graphical Microsoft Windows screen, or the DOS command prompt (see below) depending on how your system has been set up.

How to exit from the DOS Shell or Windows

Most PCs sold today are pre-installed with DOS and Windows. Also, often these machines are customised to automatically start the DOS shell or Windows after you have switched ON your machine. We will look at how do achieve this customisation yourself, later in the book, if it has not already been done for you.

For now though, if you are confronted with one of the graphical environments straight after powering-up and you wish to get out of it, do one of the following:

1.   Click on the File Menu at the top with your mouse. A pull-down menu will then be displayed. Click on the Exit option near the bottom.

2.   If you don't have a mouse, press Alt+F to display the pull-down menu. Then just type X.

3.   Press Alt+F4 keys.

4.   Just press the F3 key - this will only work if you want to exit from the DOS shell. It is not valid for Windows.

What is the DOS Command Prompt?

Once you exit either from Windows or the DOS shell you are at the DOS command prompt. It looks something like this:

```
C>  _
```

The DOS command prompt is in fact a prompt for you to type a DOS command. It is also sometimes called the *System Prompt.*

The letter C is the current disk drive. It can be A or B, if you log on to one of these floppy disk drives. Drive C is usually the hard disk. It is also the default drive when you power up. Sometimes you can use drive D if you have a second hard disk or a CD-ROM drive installed. Other letters are not really used unless your PC is linked to a network.

The greater-than symbol (or >) just tells you that this is where you should type your DOS commands. The small flashing dash after it is called a *cursor*. This is where the first character you type will appear. The cursor will also move to the right automatically, ready to receive the next character, and so on. This invisible line where DOS commands are typed is referred to as the *Command Line*.

Typing on the Command line

Try typing something on the Command line. For example:

```
C> good morning
```

If you have made a mistake in typing or you have changed your mind, press the backspace key to delete characters to the left. The back arrow key too can be used to delete text. You will notice characters disappearing one at a time from the right.

When you are happy with the text you have typed on the command line, press

It is only then that DOS will try to interpret your command or instruction. If you had typed the text "good morning" as shown in our example, DOS will issue the message:

```
Bad command or file name
```

There is no harm done to your computer for typing something totally meaningless to DOS as shown here. So don't be scared. You cannot damage the information stored on your computer or cause the circuitry inside to blow-up. That usually only happens in science-fiction films!

You have to, however, type a valid command for DOS to obey and execute it. You will learn most of these commands in this book. Once you have learned these, you will feel much more confident about using your computer.

Instead of typing a DOS command, if you had typed a program name, DOS will automatically load that program in memory and run it. For example, to run the word-processor WordPerfect, type:

```
C> wp
```

Resetting and turning "OFF" your computer

Inevitably you will want to switch off your computer. Although this is simple enough by just flicking or pressing the ON/OFF switch there are a few precautions you should take before hitting this button:

Never switch OFF whilst you are using a software application. You may corrupt the software or your own information. Always exit to the DOS command prompt from whatever you were using before switching off.

If there is a floppy disk inserted in a drive then remove it. Also ensure that the floppy disk drive light is not lit when you remove the disk to confirm that information is not being read from the disk or written to it.

First switch off all the peripherals before switching off your PC. This will typically include items like your printer. You probably don't have to worry about your monitor - nowadays most are powered through the main power supply in your system unit - and will switch off automatically when you switch off your PC.

Don't switch your computer ON straight after you have switched it off. Wait about a minute!

Some people leave their computer ON all the time or at least for very long periods. This is really OK. Nowadays a PC does not consume too much power and secondly, switching your PC OFF and ON again too frequently may reduce its life.

Sometimes instead of switching the machine OFF and ON again, you can just reset it. This is a safer alternative and it can be used when your keyboard is locked or your display looks funny.

Some computers have a RESET button, so just press this to restart the system. You should watch out for the same warnings given as for switching OFF your computer.

If you don't have a reset button then press the following keys together:

Anything in memory that has not been saved will be lost forever when you reset or switch off your computer.

Some Basic
DOS Commands

In this chapter you will learn ....

➤ The DOS command structure

➤ How to display a directory of files on disk

➤ How to display the contents of a specific file

➤ How to access another disk drive and another directory

➤ How to alter the date and time inside the computer clock

➤ How to find out which version of DOS you have

➤ How to clear the screen

➤ How to obtain online help on any DOS command

REMEMBER

All DOS commands have a structure or a format that is useful to know. Each command is really made up of up to three parts.

They are:

-     Command
-     Parameters
-     Options or switches

For example, try typing the DOS command:

```
C> dir a: /w
```

This command will display a directory of files on your disk. 'dir' is the command part, 'a:' is parameter and '/w' is the option or switch part.

First, the 'a:' parameter indicates that you want to see the files in the floppy disk in your A drive. You can leave this parameter out and it will display the directory of your current disk which is C (or the hard disk).

The '/w' switch will display the directory in wide format, occupying up to five columns. Again, you could issue the 'dir' command without the /w option but you'll find that if you have many files, some of them will scroll off the top of the screen when they are displayed in the default single-column format.

The problem with the /w switch is that it will only display the file names on your disk. There is no room to display the size and the date/time of creation of all the files too. Therefore, use the /p switch to display the directory of files in single-column with the related information too, but when a screen-full of files is displayed, there will be a pause and a message 'Press any key to continue ...'. Usually, people press the spacebar key - probably because it is the largest key on your keyboard, but you could literally press 'any' key. The next scren-full of files will then be displayed, and so on.

The parameters and switches are not always compulsory. For some DOS commands, however, parameters are essential. Without them the command simply cannot work. A good example of this is the COPY command. You have to specify the file to copy and where to copy it. The COPY command on its own is meaningless! We will discuss this command in detail later in the book.

Displaying the directory

The DIR command can be issued in all of these varying forms as we have just seen:

```
DIR              DIR A:
DIR /W           DIR A: /W
DIR /P           DIR A: /P
```

The output will vary depending on which switch is used. If the /w switch is not used, certain information for each file is displayed as shown:

```
Volume in drive C is CS_V0101
Volume Serial Number is 3238-10F7
Directory of C:\

COMMAND  COM  47845     09/04/91   5:00
DOS      <DIR>          04/12/91  10:04
DOS1     PCX  33344     31/01/92  20:42
WINDOWS <DIR>           04/12/91  10:04
CONFIG   SYS    191     18/09/91   8:57
AUTOEXEC BAT    168     22/01/92  17:06
       4 file(s) 81548 bytes
       35852288 bytes free
```

The first thing to notice is that entries with <DIR> symbol are not files but sub-directory names in the current directory.

Usually, the file name is in two parts: the first is the name itself of up to 8 characters and the second bit is the file type or extension. This is 3 characters long.

Then the size of the file is given in bytes (number of characters), followed by the date and time of creation for each file.

Displaying the contents of a file

After finding out which files you have on your disk how do you look inside a particular file and see the information it contains?

For most files you cannot really read the contents directly from DOS. This is because many files are part of the software you have installed on your computer and they are deliberately protected by the software publishers. Other files, even though you may have created them, can only be displayed or printed through the software you used to create them in the first place. All of these files will just display meaningless gobbledygook if you tried to read them!

You can, however, read a pure text file (also called an ASCII file). For example to display a file called, readme.txt, type:

```
C> type readme.txt
```

If the file is too long and some of it scrolls off at the top of the screen, then there are a few alternatives:

The simplest way is to press:

Keep the Control key pressed and tap on the "S" key to pause the display. To display some more text or to un-pause the display press Ctrl and S keys again.

This method is the simplest but not very reliable - you may miss some of the text if you're not quick enough with pressing Ctrl+S. A much better method is using the *more* filter:

```
C> type readme.txt | more
```

The first example, as shown above, uses the "bar" character. This is usually found on the same key as the blackslash (\ ) character and so you'll have to keep the shift key depressed before typing this character. Note that there is a space on either side of the bar. Then type the "more" keyword. This is a special filter program that reads the whole file but only displays one screen at a time to you. After displaying a screen it displays a prompt "___ more ___" and when you have read the information on this screen, press any key from the keyboard (usually the spacebar) to see the next screen-full and so on, until the whole file is displayed.

Another way to achieve the same results is to use the "more" filter slightly differently:

```
C> more < readme.txt
```

Changing disk drives

To access another disk drive, type the letter designated to represent the drive followed by a colon. For example, to access the A (or first) floppy disk drive, type:

```
C> a:
```

Ensure that you have inserted a floppy disk into your drive A before accessing it.

To access the C (hard disk) drive again, type:

```
A> c:
```

Changing the directory

You may not find the file you're looking for by just changing disk drives. This is because DOS uses directories to divide information stored on your computer. Think of disks as a way of physically dividing information stored and directories as a way of logically dividing this information further.

We will come back to this important subject later, but for now remember that the main directory is called the *root* (represented by a backslash "\" symbol) and all other directories are sub-directories. A sub-directory from the root can also have other sub-directories and so on.

This is all best illustrated with examples:

```
C> cd \accounts
```

Changes the directory to accounts which exists directly under the root.

```
C> cd \accounts\data
```

Changes the directory to data which exists under accounts. Note that the whole "path" needs to be specified (i.e all the directories that exist in between to get to the target directory).

```
C> cd \
```

Changes the directory to the root.

The CD command is really a short version of CHDIR command, standing for Change Directory. However, it is easier to use CD because there is less to type!

Changing the computer date and time

Just like setting the date and time in any modern electronic appliance, like a fax, video player and even a microwave, you can set the correct date and time on your PC or just check it! Your PC has a built-in clock and a calendar that is working even when you switch the machine off. To check or change the date, type:

```
C> date
```

The system will then display the current date:

```
Current date is Tue 27-04-1993
Enter new date (dd-mm-yyyy): _
```

To reset the date to 2nd February 1994, type:

```
02-02-1994
```

However, if the date is correct and you don't want to change it, just press the Enter key. To check the current time, type:

```
C> time
```

The computer may display:

```
Current time is 10:24:57.85a
Enter new time: _
```

To set the time to 1.35p.m. say, type:

```
13:35
```

The computer has a 24-hour clock. You can choose to type just the hour and minutes, even though the display also gives seconds and hundredth of a second.

To change the date or time regardless of the current setting, simply type the appropriate command followed by a space and then the new date or time, as shown above but all in one command.

DOS versions

If you don't know or don't remember which version of DOS you have installed on your computer, just type:

```
C> ver
```

and DOS will tell you whether it's version 2.0, 2.1, 3.1, 3.2, 4.0, 5.0, 6.0 etc. At the time of writing this book MS-DOS 6.2 was the current release.

Note that the decimal digits are important in version numbers. As with any other software version number, an increase in the first decimal digit represents a minor but important upgrade to the package e.g. DOS 3.2 enhanced the product with a few improvements not present in the previous DOS 3.1.

An increase in the second decimal digit represents a very minor improvement. For example, there is virtually no difference between DOS 4.01 and DOS 4.00. These upgrades are not really planned by software publishers but have become necessary to rectify errors in the software.

Finally, a change in the main version number is certainly planned and represents a major upgrade. Quite often this upgrade is a rewrite of large chunks of the software. It should contain substantial improvements and extra features. For example, DOS 6.0 is a major upgrade from DOS 5.0.

Clearing the screen

Another short command which some may use is the CLS command to clear the screen.

This is especially useful if you have sensitive information displayed on the screen and someone walks into the room. Quickly type:

```
C> cls
```

and the whole screen will clear.

Help on a DOS command

If you have DOS version 5 or higher, you can use the HELP command followed by a DOS command to obtain information on how to use the specific command - the parameters and options you can use will also be displayed. For example:

```
C> help dir or   dir /?
```

HELP on its own will display all commands alphabetically.

The DOS Command Prompt

In this chapter you will learn ....

- How to make the DOS command prompt more helpful

- To type at the DOS command prompt

- Useful editing techniques

- How to cancel a command

- Difference between Internal and External commands

The DOS command prompt is where you type DOS commands, as seen in the first chapter. This prompt is a way the computer is informing you that it is waiting for your input. You can of course ignore the request and do nothing. However, inside your computer there is a little program, running all the time and checking if you have entered a command for it to process.

Also note that the DOS command prompt is as old as DOS itself. It has stood the test of time and remained throughout the development of DOS and all it's versions. Having said this, you may still feel a little uncomfortable working at the DOS prompt. You may not find it very user-friendly! If you have DOS version 4 or higher, then you can use the DOS shell instead (see Chapter 5). Although, you'll find that some of the functions cannot be performed through the shell and it is sometimes much easier to simply type a DOS command at the prompt. For these reasons it is well worth being familiar with the DOS prompt and the way to issue commands here.

The Prompt command

When you are moving around different directories at the command prompt, it is difficult to know which directory/sub-directory you are using at any time. The PROMPT command can be used to change the DOS command prompt and give you this information. Type:

```
C> prompt $p$g
```

Now, rather than just seeing the disk drive letter, the command prompt is changed to display the current directory too. For example, when you are at the root directory, the command prompt will look like:

```
C:\>
```

The \ again indicating that it is the root directory. If you change to the WP directory, the command prompt changes to:

```
C:\WP>
```

Changing the directory again to PERSONAL will show:

```
C:\WP\PERSONAL>
```

It is possible to change the command prompt in many different ways by using other parameters for the PROMPT command. For example, $d will always show today's date and $t, the current time. Any special name or text after the PROMPT command will be simply displayed as part of the command prompt:

```
C:\> prompt yes master?
```

The most useful type of command prompt, however, is one that displays the current directory with the pg parameter. The PROMPT command with this parameter is usually included in the AUTOEXEC.BAT file (see later) so that it is permanent.

To revert back to the default command prompt, C>, just type the PROMPT command without any parameters.

Typing commands at the Prompt

Use your keyboard to type DOS commands at the DOS command prompt. As you type, the cursor will move to the right a character at a time. Press the Enter key once you complete typing the full command and want DOS to obey it.

If you have made a mistake in typing, press the Backspace key. This will delete characters one at a time from the right. Simply re-type the bit that was incorrect and the rest of the command.

If you want to delete the whole line, press the Esc key or Ctrl+C keys.

If you want to issue the same command again or alter it slightly and then issue it again, rather than to type it all again, just press the F3 key. This will display the last command at the command prompt as if you had typed it in.

Using DOSkey for DOS version 5 and higher

Normally, DOS only provides very basic editing facilities. You can only retrieve the last command. If you find yourself doing a lot of editing and having to re-type previously issued commands, use DOSkey to reduce the number of keystrokes.

DOSkey is just a program that you can install in your computer's temporary memory. However, you will need to have one of the more recent versions (version 5 upwards) of DOS to be able to use it. To install DOSkey, simply type its name at the prompt:

```
C:\> doskey
```

Now, some of the most useful keys you can use to simplify editing including re-issuing previous commands are:

Arrow Keys. Keep pressing the UP arrow key to display previous commands issued or the DOWN arrow key to reverse the sequence in which DOS commands are displayed. When you find the one that you want to use again, simply press the Enter key. If you want to modify the command slightly before re-issuing it, use the LEFT and RIGHT arrow keys to edit it.

F7 Key. This will display a batch of DOS commands that have been used so far. Each of these commands can be accessed by UP/DOWN arrow keys (as discussed above). Also, any one command can be accessed directly (see F9 key).

F9 Key. The display from F7 key also displays a unique command number in front of each command. Press F9 and then one of these command numbers to re-issue the appropriate command.

Cancelling a command

Occasionally, you may want to cancel a DOS command that has already been issued. Perhaps it's because it is taking a long time to complete the command. For example, when a directory listing or a display of a text file on the screen seems to be taking forever.

The best way to cancel the command in operation is to press:

 +

You'll then see displayed on your screen, "^C" followed by a DOS command prompt.

The ^ symbol is called a *caret* or a *hat*. You should not type this symbol. It is displayed when you press the "control" key in combination with another character.

As an alternative to pressing Ctrl+C keys you can press the Break key if you have it on your keyboard (or even Ctrl+Break).

Don't press the Reset button or switch off your computer just to cancel a DOS command.

Internal and External commands

There are two types of DOS commands you can issue at the DOS command prompt: internal and external. Internal commands are all contained within a file called COMMAND.COM. This file is loaded automatically into memory when DOS is loaded. Examples of internal commands include:

COPY, DEL, DIR, TYPE

These commands can be issued from any disk drive or directory because they are in the computer's memory.

External commands, however, are not in memory to start with. They reside as separate files on your disk; one for each command. When you issue an external command, the relevant file has to be located and loaded into memory from disk - just like when you want to run a program. Examples include:

BACKUP, CHKDSK, FORMAT, UNDELETE

Both internal and external commands are covered in this book.
Chapter 17 also lists all major DOS commands and tells you
whether they are internal or external.

Basic
File Operations

In this chapter you will learn ....

➤ How to copy and duplicate files

➤ How to move files

➤ How to rename files

➤ How to delete and undelete files

➤ How to print files

Files are basic units of information that DOS manages. All your work is stored in a number of files. Some examples of files you may create and work with include word processor documents, spreadsheet forecasts and graphic illustrations. Even software products like WordPerfect and Lotus 1-2-3 that you may purchase consists of several files and even DOS itself includes a number of files.

Therefore being able to work with files is very important and this is largely what DOS is all about.

Copying just one file

Copying a file is easy with DOS. Using the COPY command, you need to know the name of the file you want to copy and where you want to copy it to (the destination). For example, to copy a file named compstep.txt from your hard disk C to a floppy disk A, type:

```
C> copy compstep.txt a:
```

This assumes that you are issuing the COPY command from the appropriate directory in your C disk. If you are not, prefix the filename with the correct path:

```
C> copy c:\general\work\compstep.txt a:
```

You could change to the appropriate directory first, using the CD command, and then issue the copy command in our first example to achieve the same result.

The path can also be specified on the other side (the destination side) of the copy command. For example,

```
C> copy myfile.doc b:\letters
```

Another trick is to copy a file to your current disk/directory from somewhere else easily by only issuing one parameter in the copy command:

```
C> copy a:sample.doc
```

This command does not have the destination-part because it takes the current disk and directory from where you issue the command as the destination. Obviously, you cannot copy a file onto itself - so you have to issue the command from a different disk or directory to where the source file is stored.

Duplicating a file

The copy command can also be used to duplicate a file:

```
C> copy myfile.doc newfile.doc
```

In this example a new file called, newfile.doc will be created and it will be identical to myfile.doc in every way except of course it will have a different name.

Copying several files

To copy several files in one operation or command, wildcards need to be used.

Wildcards are special characters which can represent any variable number of characters (*) or any single character (?). For example, DOS?.DOC can represent the following files:

DOS1.DOC
DOS2.DOC
DOS3.DOC

But DOS10.DOC will not be selected. However, DOS*.DOC will select all files starting with DOS and DOS??.DOC will select DOS10.DOC but not the three files listed above.

You can use wildcards in the name and the extension part of the filename. So to copy all compstep files, regardless of the extension:

```
C> copy compstep.* a:
```

To copy all the files from a floppy disk onto your hard disk, type:

```
A> copy *.* c:
```

This command is commonly referred to as the star-dot-star variety and it is used very frequently.

Another variation on the same command is to use it to copy the full contents of a directory to a floppy disk:

```
C> copy c:\temp\*.* a:
```

Using COPY to create new files

Yes! there is even a way of creating new files quickly using the COPY command. Perhaps you want to try this technique to create files used in this book so that you can experiment with the commands described. To create a new file, type:

```
C> copy con compstep.txt
```

con is short for console or keyboard. This command will copy whatever is typed next on the keyboard to a new file called compstep.txt.

Type whatever you want after issuing this command and then when you have finished, press F6 or Ctrl+Z (^Z will be displayed on the screen) followed by the Enter key. This will create the new file.

Moving files

Sometimes there is a need to move files instead of copying them. For example, when you want to reorganise various files into their appropriate directories or disks.

There are two ways of achieving this:

First, is to copy the file to your new destination using the COPY command just described. Then, delete the original file from the disk (see the DEL command later in this chapter). These two commands (COPY followed by DEL) will effectively enable you to move one or more files.

The second method can be achieved in just one command but you need to have DOS version 6 or higher. These versions have a new command for moving files and there are no prizes for guessing what this command is called - yes quite simply it's called the MOVE command and here's how it's used:

```
C> move myfile.doc \windows
```

Here myfile.doc is moved from the current directory to the windows directory.

You can rename the file at the same time as moving it by typing the new name in the destination parameter of the command.

You can move several files in the same operation by typing their names separated by spaces.

The move command can be also used to rename a directory. Just type the current directory name followed by the new directory name after the move command.

If files with same names exist in the destination directory or disk, they'll be over-written.

Renaming files

If you want to just rename a file without making a copy of it, use the REN command. Type:

```
C> ren compstep.txt compstep.new
```

The first filename you type after the REN command will be renamed to the second filename. If the file you want to rename is in another directory you can either issue the command after changing the directory or specifying the path in the command:

```
C> ren a:\backup\letters\fred john
```

The file name 'fred' is renamed to 'john'. You don't need to type the path again for the new file name. You can also use wildcards to rename several files too:

```
C> ren *.txt *.old
```

All files in the current directory ending with .txt will be renamed with a new file extension, .old.

You cannot rename all files - in other words you cannot use *.* (star-dot-star) in one operation. As a general rule only a group of matching files can be renamed in one command. The same wildcards in the same position need to be specified for both the current and the new filename.

Deleting files

To delete files use either DEL or ERASE commands. They are both exactly the same. DEL is easier because there is less to type and so we'll use it here:

```
C> del todo.lst
```

Type the file name after the DEL command to delete it. You will not get any warning or message. The file will just disappear - unless of course it does not exist; in which case you will get a message:

```
"File not found"
```

You can delete files from another disk or directory by prefixing the file name with disk/path. To delete several files use wildcards as before.

If you were to, however, try and delete all the files on a disk by using the star-dot-star wildcard, like:

```
C> del *.*
```

you will see a warning message:

```
All files in directory will be deleted!
Are you sure (Y/N)?
```

This is displayed because deleting all the files from a directory is considered a drastic step. Think twice before pressing "Y" for Yes followed by the Enter key. You will loose everything from the directory.

Undeleting files

If you have accidently deleted one or more important files it may still not be the end of the world - but only if you have DOS 5 or a later version of DOS. You may be able to recover them with the UNDELETE command.

There is no guarantee that all files that are deleted can be recovered. If you should need to use the UNDELETE command, use it as quickly as possible after the DEL command and before any other commands are issued. This is because once a file is deleted its space can be used to store other files you create or copy. If this happens then even UNDELETE cannot help you.

The UNDELETE command reverses the DEL command and should be used in exactly the same way as the DEL command. For example:

```
C> undelete impfile.exe
```

DOS will then display some technical information that you don't need to worry about. It will also list the filename(s) you want undeleted and whether that's possible. If it is possible, you'll have to type "Y" against each file you want undeleted and also type the first letter of the filename replacing the "?" prefix.

```
C> undelete /list
```

This will list all files that can be recovered.

```
C> undelete /all
```

This will recover all deleted files without asking you to confirm the undeletion for individual files.

For more information on Undeleting files, see Chapter 15 - Securing against Loss of Data.

Printing files

You should only print text files directly from DOS. If you're not sure that a particular file is a text file, use the TYPE command to display the file on screen. If you can read it, it's a text file. If you see gobbledygook or funny characters, then you will not be able to print the file successfully either.

Most files should be printed using the software that created them. These include word processor, spreadsheet and graphics files.

To print text files from DOS, type:

```
C> print readme.txt
```

Another easy way to print text files is to use the COPY command:

```
C> copy readme.txt prn
```

This will copy the readme.txt file to your printer, designated by prn.

Ensure that paper is loaded and your printer is switched to on-line before you issue commands to print.

After your file has been printed, you may have to switch your printer to off-line mode and then press the form feed button to eject the last page. Laser printers will often not eject a page that is not fully printed and there are no more pages to print. Therefore to force an ejection through DOS, type:

```
C> echo Ctrl + l > prn
```

The above command (echo) should be typed first followed by a space and then, press the Ctrl (control) key and while still holding it down, tap on the letter L. You'll notice ^L (a hat symbol prefixing L) displayed on the screen. Then hold down the shift key and press > (greater-than symbol). This symbol redirects output, in this case to the printer, and it will be covered in detail later in Chapter 12. The final bit is to just type prn followed by the Enter key to send the command to DOS and you should notice a sheet of paper ejecting from your printer.

You don't have to use DOS at all for printing files. Most word processors and editors can do this too. You also have the advantage with these products to be able to view the file before printing it. If you have DOS version 5 or higher, you can use an editor program included in the package, called EDIT, to print files. See Chapter 13 for more information.

You can also print whatever is displayed on the screen by just pressing the Print Screen button found on most keyboards. If this does not work, press and hold down the shift key and then press the Print Screen button (sometimes abbreviated on the key cap as PrtSc or Print Scrn).

Using the
DOS Shell

In this chapter you will learn ....

> How to start and exit from the DOS shell

> How to use various parts of the shell including the Help system

> How to customise the shell to different colours and resolutions

> How to split the screen to see files from other disks or directories

> How to copy, move, delete and rename single files or groups of files

> How to find lost files even when you don't remember the full filename

> How to use other programs from the shell

The DOS shell is an easy-to-use interface between you and DOS. It was first introduced in version 4.0 of DOS and then improved by Microsoft in version 5.0. The shell has remained the same in version 6.0 and 6.2. In this chapter we will look at how the shell can be used to perform essential DOS functions.

Essentially, the DOS shell is a Graphical User Interface (commonly abbreviated as GUI - pronounced 'gooey'). It replaces the DOS command prompt and the command line. Instead of the almost blank screen and the command prompt, a full screen is displayed with names of common applications, files and directories. These are all prefixed with little icons (or pictures) that give clues to what the items may contain. It also provides 'pull-down' menus and mouse support to make using your computer much easier.

If you are familiar with Microsoft Windows, then the DOS shell offers a similar environment. In fact, many of the functions covered here can also be performed using the Windows File Manager.

The greatest advantage of using the shell is that you will not have to remember or type commands at the DOS command prompt. However, the shell will not allow you to perform all functions available within DOS and also you really do need a mouse to use it - although it is possible to use the shell from the keyboard, it was not designed to be used in that way.

If you prefer to work from the shell some of the time and also at the DOS command prompt at other times, then there isn't a problem - because there is a facility within the shell to allow you to temporarily exit to the DOS command prompt. Also, you'll be able to quickly return to the DOS shell exactly at the point you left.

Starting the Shell

When you install DOS you will have the option to run the shell automatically on startup. If you do not choose this option, you can still activate the shell from the DOS command prompt by typing:

```
C> dosshell
```

After you press the Enter key, the DOS shell is loaded and you'll see the following main screen displayed:

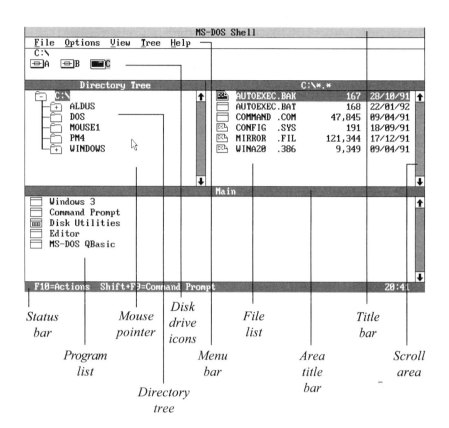

Exiting from the Shell

To exit permanently from the shell and to return back to the DOS command prompt, click on File at the top left corner and then click on the Exit option from the File pull-down menu displayed.

Alternatively, just press F3 or Alt+F4 key combinations to exit from the shell.

Main areas of the Shell

You will see three main areas within the shell. They are, starting from upper left: Directory Tree, File List to the right of it, and Main at the bottom.

The easiest way to access a particular area is to click anywhere inside it with your mouse button. If you do not have a mouse, you can press the Tab key on your keyboard to toggle between the three areas. You will always know which area is selected because the title bar for that area will be highlighted.

Directory tree

In this area you can see the structure of all directories. Directories are logical sections on the disk to store information or files. Therefore, you may decide to have a directory for all your word processor documents and another one for all your accounts data files. The word processor directory may consist of other sub-directories, say one for storing all your business letters and another one for your personal letters. The word processor software itself can also have it's own directory. We will cover directories in more detail later in the book.

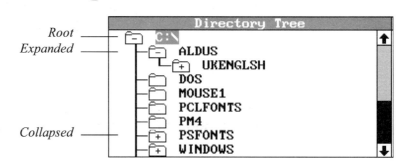

For now it is sufficient to understand how the shell displays directories. The small boxes in front of the directory names are called *folder icons*. If there is a '+' symbol inside a folder, you can click on it with your mouse button to see and expand the particular directory into sub-directories. Alternatively, type the key '+'. The selected directory will then expand to one level and the '+' will change to a '-' symbol. If you now type '-' or click on it's folder icon, the directory will collapse again.

Type '*' to expand a directory to all its levels or type Ctrl+* to expand all directories to all levels.

HANDY TIP

File list

The File list area will display all files contained within the particular directory or subdirectory selected in the Directory tree. To select a directory, click on it with your mouse or use the cursor arrow keys on your keyboard.

Main area

The Main area at the bottom of the screen lists programs that may be used frequently. Double-click on any one of them with your mouse (or select them by using arrow keys followed by the Enter key) to execute or run the program. The programs supplied with DOS and those that you will see after installing it are:

Command Prompt: allows you to temporarily exit to the DOS command prompt. Here you can type any DOS commands required - perhaps to perform functions not supported from within the shell. Then, to return back to the shell, just type:

```
C> exit
```

Editor: a text editor used to create or edit files. These files include important DOS files like the AUTOEXEC.BAT or CONFIG.SYS (see Chapter 13).

MS-DOS QBasic: a BASIC programming language allowing you to write your own programs if you want to.

Disk Utilities: consists of several different programs. You will be able to format disks, copy and backup files and even undelete files that have been deleted previously.

If you use a particular program often enough, like a word processor for example, you can create a program group/item of your own to appear here (see Chapter 10 on how to do this). Then, everytime you want to use the wordprocessor, simply double-click on this entry.

You can also run several programs simultaneously in the Main area. This is achieved by a feature introduced in version 5 called the *Task swapper* - discussed in Chapter 10.

Scrolling

All the three main display areas just described also have little scroll areas to the right of them. These allow you to scroll up and down when the information to display cannot fit into the small area reserved. Just click on the up-arrow or the down-arrow to scroll gently in either direction. Alternatively, click anywhere between the two arrows to scroll directly to that part of the list. You can also scroll by using the arrow keys and PageUp, PageDown, Home and End keys.

Disk drive icons

The disk drive icons are just above the Directory tree. You should see disk drive C highlighted by default. To access or use other drives just click on them with your mouse.

Alternatively, press Ctrl+A to access drive A, Ctrl+B to access drive B and so on. Once a disk drive is selected, you can also select other adjacent drives by using the left and right arrow keys.

Pull-down menus

Above the disk drive icons there are five pull-down menu options. These allow you to perform various common tasks.

Just click on them to use them. You can also access them by pressing the F10 or the Alt key. This will just highlight the first menu option (the File menu). You need to use the arrow keys to access other adjacent menu options and then press the Enter key to 'pull-down' or expand options under the main highlighted menu.

You can also press the Alt key and the first letter of the menu option, say Alt+V, to access the View menu directly. Once your pull-down menu is displayed, you can select a function from it by clicking on it with your mouse, using Up/Down arrow keys to highlight the option and pressing Enter, or by just pressing the underlined letter of the option you require. If you've selected the wrong menu or function, press the Esc key to backout. The main menus and their functions are:

File: enables you to manage files (copy, delete, rename - see later), run programs and even create new directories to store files. Sometimes, some options from pull-down menus are dimmed (on colour screens they may be displayed in a different colour). These options cannot be selected because you have to do something else first before they are valid. For example, if you have not selected the File list area and highlighted one or more files, options like Move, Copy, Rename and so on, will be dimmed because

```
Open
Run...
Print
Associate...
Search...
View File Contents    F9

Move...                F7
Copy...                F8
Delete...              Del
Rename...
Change Attributes...

Create Directory...

Select All
Deselect All

Exit                   Alt+F4
```

they all need files as a pre-requisite. Also, the File menu looks completely different when you are in the Main program area - try it and see!

Options: enables you to tailor the DOS shell to the way you prefer to work. It allows you to change the display (see later), choose whether you want to be prompted to confirm deletion of files and what information you prefer to see displayed about files.

View: allows you to split the screen to display two file lists (so you can compare the entries from two disks say), display program list, file list or both. It also allows you to re-display the screen to show new entries.

Tree: shows you the directory structure. You can "expand" or "collapse" directories or subdirectories. The Tree menu option is not displayed when the Main area is active because it is not relevant.

Help: displays online help on your screen (explained next).

Getting help

There is an online help facility included in the DOS shell. It can save you time looking up the relevant information from your DOS reference manual. Click on the Help menu with your mouse or just press Alt+H to activate it.

```
 Help
┌──────────────────┐
│ Index            │
│ Keyboard         │
│ Shell Basics     │
│ Commands         │
│ Procedures       │
│ Using Help       │
├──────────────────┤
│ About Shell      │
└──────────────────┘
```

Choose Index for a listing of all Help topics, Keyboard for key-combinations to use with the shell, Shell Basics to learn some of the features already covered in this chapter, Commands to get help on specific menu commands and Procedures to obtain more detailed instructions on how to perform various functions.

Using Help will teach you how to use the Help system itself and About Shell will show you the version number and the Microsoft copyright.

HANDY TIP

If you highlight a menu or a specific command within it and press F1, you will get help specifically on that subject. This is called *Context-Sensitive Help*.

Changing the screen resolution and colours

If you select the Options menu you will see an item called Display. Click on it to select it. A dialog box of screen modes will be displayed:

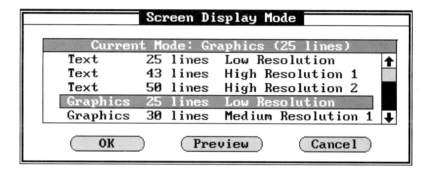

Select either one of the text modes or graphics modes. You can preview the display chosen by clicking on the Preview button at the bottom. If you like it, then click on OK or press Enter to make the change permanent.

If you have a colour monitor, you can also choose Colours from the Options menu. Select and preview the colour you like from a scrollable list in exactly the same way as you would from the Display dialog box just described.

Viewing files

The shell provides several ways of viewing files you have. You can view most files and the related information from the View menu. For example, Single File list will show just the directory tree on the left and the file list on the right. The program list at the bottom disappears to make more room to see more files at the same time.

Click on Dual file list option from the View menu to duplicate the file list as shown below:

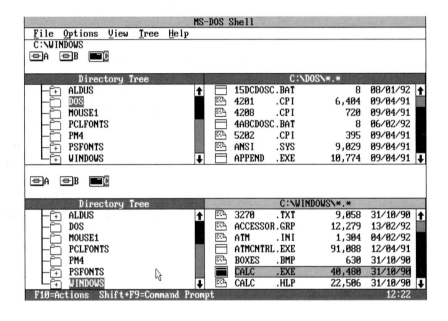

This display makes copying or moving files from one disk or directory to another very easy - because both your source and destination drive/directory are displayed at the same time on one screen (these operations are covered a little later in this chapter). Hence this type of display is also sometimes referred to as a *split-screen* display.

You can select the appropriate file list simply by clicking anywhere in its area. Also, you'll notice that even the disk drive icons are duplicated on the second file list. So you could click on say disk drive A from the second file list to display files from your floppy disk A in the second file list. Make sure however, that you have first inserted a disk in drive A.

Both Single and Dual file lists also display the directory tree on the left. You can click on another directory name from one of the lists in a dual file list, as shown in our example, to see files present there without losing the display showing your main files in the other file list.

You can also display files from all directories at once by choosing All Files from the View menu. You'll see that as well as the file name, size and date, this display also shows the time each file was created or changed.

On the left of the 'All Files' display, there is more detailed information on the selected file, its directory and also on the disk the file resides. For example, disk information includes the size, number of files and directories present, and the amount of space still available or free on the disk.

To see this same detailed file information from other file views, select a file and then select Show information from the Options menu.

Selecting files

Many of the functions or commands that operate on files need to have file(s) selected as a pre-requisite. To just select one file, we know that you simply click on it or use the arrow keys to highlight it from the file list.

But what if you want to select several files? One technique you can use is called *Shift-clicking*. This is used to select a consecutive block of files. Click on the first file you want to select. Then, press the Shift key and, whilst still holding it down, click on the last file you want selected from the list. You'll notice then that all the files selected, from the first to the last in the consecutive block, will be highlighted.

☐	15DCDOSC.BAT	8	08/01/92
☐	17D9DOSC.BAT	8	19/02/92
▇	1A21DOSC.BAT	8	19/02/92
▤	4201 .CPI	6,404	09/04/91
▤	4208 .CPI	720	09/04/91
▇	4A8CDOSC.BAT	8	06/02/92
▤	5202 .CPI	395	09/04/91
▤	ANSI .SYS	9,029	09/04/91
▇	APPEND .EXE	10,774	09/04/91

Shift+click method

If you want to select non-adjacent files, use Ctrl+click. Whilst pressing and holding down the Ctrl key, click on files required from the file list.

☐	DISKCOPY.COM	11,793	09/04/91
▤	DISPLAY .SYS	15,792	09/04/91
▤	DOSHELP .HLP	5,651	09/04/91
▇	DOSKEY .COM	5,883	09/04/91
☐	DOSSHELL.COM	4,623	09/04/91
☐	DOSSHELL.EXE	235,484	09/04/91
▤	DOSSHELL.GRB	4,421	09/04/91
▤	DOSSHELL.HLP	161,763	09/04/91
▤	DOSSHELL.INI	18,025	11/03/92

Control+click method

Using the Ctrl+click method you're not even restricted to selecting files from just one directory. If you choose Select Across Directories from the Options menu, then you can Ctrl+click several files from different directories.

Copying and Moving files

Copying and moving files is a frequent requirement for all users. There are two basic ways of performing these operations using the shell.

The first is by using a pull-down menu. Highlight a file or group of files to be copied by selecting them using one of the techniques just described above. Then click on the File menu and select Copy from its pull-down menu.

The 'Copy File' dialog box will be displayed and inside this box the file(s) to be copied are displayed within the 'From:' box. Specify the destination to where you want the file(s) copied in the 'To:' box. You can specify any disk drive and/or directory here. You can even specify another filename if you want to give the copy of your file a different name. Then click on the OK button to start the copy operation.

To move files, the operation is exactly the same same as copying, except choose Move from the File menu.

The second method of copying or moving files is easier and more intuitive. First select a file or a group of files from the file list.

HANDY TIP

If you press the Ctrl+/ keys, it is possible to select all files as shown in our example below:

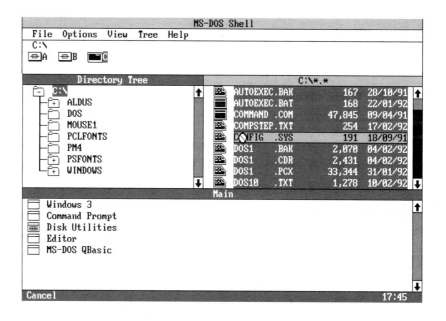

Then, if you want to move all these files to say floppy disk A, click anywhere in the file list and hold the left mouse button down after having made a selection of files to copy. Then drag the mouse pointer to drive A icon near the top. You will see the mouse arrowhead change to ⬡ and as you drag the mouse over the directory tree it changes to 🖵 .

You will be asked to confirm the mouse operation. Then, files will be copied one at a time to your destination. A box showing the status will appear on your screen too so that you'll always know how many files have been copied so far.

To move files instead of copying them, follow the same procedure except hold down the Alt key as you drag the mouse pointer from the file list to a disk drive icon or a directory name.

If you want to copy or move files to a destination you cannot see, then display a dual file list (as described in Viewing files) and access the destination directory from the second file list. Then follow the same mouse-dragging procedure described by dragging files from one file list (the source) to the second file list (destination).

There is, however, a slight difference when dragging files between two file lists - instead of copying them you'll in fact be moving them. If you want to force a copy, then hold down the Ctrl key as you perform the mouse operation.

Renaming and Deleting files

To rename a file, first highlight the file you want to rename by clicking on it from the file list. Then select Rename from the File menu. A dialog box displaying your selected filename will appear. Type the new filename in the New name box and press the Enter key or click on the OK button. Your file is now renamed to the new name specified.

To delete a file or a group of files, select one or more of them from the file list and then select Delete from the File menu. A dialog box asking you to confirm deletion is displayed if you have kept the default 'Confirm on Delete' status on.

The 'Confirm on Delete' status and others can be altered by selecting the Confirmation option from the Options menu. It is recommended that you keep all these confirmations set on. The others are 'Confirm on Replace' and 'Confirm on Mouse Operation'.

Sometimes, even if you are asked to confirm deletions, you can still accidently delete files you really had no intention of deleting. If this happens, use the Undelete program introduced in version 5. Click on Disk Utilities from the Main program area in the shell. Then click on the Undelete option.

Finding lost files

It is very easy to search for a filename you cannot find using the shell. Just choose Search from the File menu and type the name of the file you're looking for in the dialog box displayed.

If you don't know the full name of the lost file, then type as much of the name as you know. Fill the rest of the name with wildcards (these are * and ? as explained in Chapter 4). For example, if you know that your file starts with CUST, type CUST*.* or CUST*.DOC if you know the file extension to be DOC. Star-dot-star (*.*) will search for all files and it is of little use. If you select 'Search entire disk' from the dialog box too, your search may take a long time. It is best to narrow down the directories the file may be in by selecting each directory in turn from the directory tree before you invoke the search function.

Starting programs from the Shell

There are several ways of starting or running programs from the shell. First, if you have gone to the trouble of setting up programs in the program list at the bottom of the shell (see Chapter 10 on how to do this exactly) then the easiest way to start a program is just to double-click on the program name with your mouse.

You can also double-click on the main program filename from the file list to run the program. The main program filename usually has a file extension of .exe or .com. Another useful technique is to select a file you want to use with your program by clicking on it with your mouse and then drag it, keeping the left mouse button depressed, to a program filename in either the file list or the program list. Your program will then start and use the file you just dropped on it!

Another quick and simple way to start a program is to just select 'Run' from the File menu and type in the name of the program you want to run.

Storing, Managing and Organising Information

In this section you will learn all about storage devices. This will include preparing your floppy disks before information can be stored on them and compressing your hard disk to allow more storage. You'll also learn how to organise your files into directories and how to manage directories. It builds on basic file management discussed in the previous section to include useful tips on good file naming habits and how to find a lost file.

CHAPTER 6

Floppy Disks
for Storage

In this chapter you will learn ....

➤ How to use floppy disks

➤ How to write-protect disks

➤ About disk types and capacities

➤ About formatting disks before they can be used

➤ About naming disks with Volume and Label commands

➤ About creating system disks, quicker formats, using lower capacity disks

➤ About duplicating and comparing disks

The 'D' in DOS stands for Disk. Most DOS commands operate on disks. They access disks to read and write files (which can be programs or your own data/information) stored.

There are two main types of disks used for storage: Floppy disk (commonly called a floppy) and a Hard disk. The Hard disk is covered in the next chapter (Chapter 7). Here we will concentrate on floppies.

What is a floppy?

A floppy disk is a long-term storage medium. It is removable and therefore you can use it to backup important information and also transfer information between PCs.

There are two sizes of floppy disks: 5¼" and 3½". The 3½" has become the dominant standard. It offers much better protection with a hard plastic casing. Most PC manufacturers now supply machines with a built-in 3½" disk drive.

A disk drive is a mechanical device used to read and write information from/to disks.

Inserting and removing a floppy

A 3½" disk has a small metallic shutter - this is the end that is inserted into the disk drive first. If you insert the wrong end or the wrong side first, it will simply not fit into the drive and so you'll soon learn how to do it right! When you push a 3½" disk correctly and completely into the drive, the drive closes automatically, ejecting a small button out. When you want to remove the disk push this button and the disk will eject out.

Never remove a disk when its drive light is on. This is when the disk is being used - information is either being read or written.

For a 5¼" disk, insert it so that the label side is on top and the other end (this end has the actual disk exposed a bit from the jacket - it is the read/write window) enters the drive first. Again, push it in all the way. However, the drive door needs to be closed manually here by turning a latch clockwise. To remove the disk turn the latch anti-clockwise and gently pull-out the disk.

Write-protecting a floppy

You will see a little plastic slider on the top right corner of a 3½" disk. This is the write-protect hole. If you push it with a ball-point nib to reveal a hole, the disk becomes write-protected. This is useful to protect important information from being over-written. For example, master disks which you buy as part of your software package should always be write-protected.

Write-protecting a 5¼" disk is exactly opposite to write-protecting a 3½" disk - you have to cover the hole (called a notch) with a sticky tab instead of revealing it.

Floppy disk storage capacities

The storage capacity of disks can be measured in bytes. One byte is equivalent to one character. A kilobyte is 1024 bytes or characters and it is abbreviated as K. A megabyte (MB) is approximately thousand kilobytes or a million bytes. The storage capacities are summarised below:

Disk Type	Description
5¼" DS/DD	360K low capacity. Used in IBM PC, XT and compatibles for DOS versions 2.0 or later
5¼" DS/HD	1.2MB high capacity. Used in IBM AT and compatibles for DOS versions 3.0 or later
3½" DS/DD	720K low capacity. Used in IBM PS/2 30 and compatibles for DOS versions 3.2 or later
3½" DS/HD	1.44MB high capacity. Used in IBM PS/2, AT and compatibles for DOS versions 3.3 or later

DS=double sided
DD=double density
HD=high density

You can also buy extended capacity (DS/ED) 3½" floppies for a higher storage capacity of up to 2.8MB.

You should match the floppy disks you buy to the storage capacity of your disk drive.

Accessing disks from disk drives

If you only have one floppy disk drive it is assigned the letter A. If you have two, the first (A) is usually on top and the second one is assigned the letter B. The letter C is reserved for the hard disk. Other letters are not usually used unless you have additional drives, or if your PC is connected to a network where you have access to several disks.

To access a disk from another drive type the drive letter (A,B or C) followed by a colon. The colon distinguishes it from a filename.

If your DOS version is between 3.0 and 5.0 you can allocate other letters to represent the standard disk drive letters with the ASSIGN command. For example:

```
C> assign a = c
```

will access drive C as A too. The ASSIGN command is removed from DOS version 6.0 though. This is not a big loss since it is not recommended you use it - you may have problems using some software if you use this command!

Formatting

Before you can use floppy disks to store information or files you have to prepare them for use. This is achieved by the FORMAT command.

FORMAT will structure the disk into concentric circles called tracks. Each pie-slice or segment through a number of tracks is called a sector.

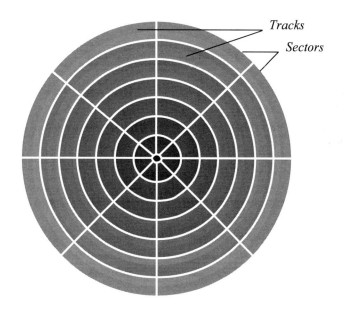

The number of tracks and sectors on a disk determines its storage capacity. FORMAT will automatically allocate the right number of these, depending on the storage capacity of your disk and the type of disk drive you have.

To format a disk in drive A say, type:

```
C> format A:
```

DOS will prompt you to insert a disk:

```
Insert new diskette for drive A:
and press ENTER when ready ...
```

After you insert the disk and press the ENTER key:

```
Checking existing disk format
saving UNFORMAT information
verifying 1.44M
        xx percent of disk formatted
```

Then the disk is formatted and the progress can be monitored from the percent figure being incremented. When its all completed, DOS will display:

```
Format complete
```

Formatting will wipe off any information you may have on the disk. So be very careful not to format disks that contain information you still require.

Naming a disk

After the disk is formatted and before the DOS command prompt is displayed, DOS will display:

```
Volume label (11 characters, ENTER for
none)?
```

The Volume label is used to name the disk. Type in a sensible name that will enable you to identify the contents of the disk at some later stage. For example, type ACCOUNTS_94 if you are going to use the disk to backup all your 1994 accounts files.

Although the Volume label is optional (you can just press ENTER to avoid it) it is well worth using. It is just like sticking a label on a music cassette you have recorded and writing a title so that you will always know what has been recorded. Of course you can also stick a paper label on the disk too so that you will know the contents even before you insert the disk in your computer!

Once you press ENTER after the Volume label prompt, DOS will display some statistics on disk space:

```
1457664 bytes total disk space
1457664 bytes available on disk

512     bytes in each allocation unit
2847    allocation units available on disk
```

Volume Serial Number is 045D-1AEA

Format another (Y/N)?

You will also be able to format another disk in the same way here if you are planning to do a few at a time. However, type 'N' to return to the DOS command prompt.

If you want to check the Volume label later for a disk, say in disk drive A, insert the disk and type:

```
C> vol a:
```

If you did not put a Volume label during the formatting of the disk and need to add it later on, or more likely change it and even delete it, use the LABEL command:

```
C> label a:ACCOUNTS_94
```

Creating a system disk

When you format a disk, it is possible to copy the main DOS system files to it too. It is useful to do this just in case there is a problem on the hard disk and you need to start your computer and DOS from a floppy disk. Therefore to create a system disk from a disk inserted in drive A, type:

```
C>  format a: /s
```

Now label your newly created system disk as 'DOS SYSTEM DISK' and keep it in a safe place.

If you want to transfer DOS to an already formatted disk, in drive A type:

```
C> sys a:
```

The above command is same as using the /S option on the FORMAT command. It will transfer all the important DOS files to your floppy disk.

However, external DOS command files will not be copied. These may be important to you in trying to recover information from the hard disk and to then format the hard disk (see Chapters 15 and 7 respectively for details on how to do this). It is recommended that you copy the following individual files using the COPY command too:

FORMAT.COM
BACKUP.EXE
RESTORE.EXE
CHKDSK.EXE

If you are using an earlier version then DOS 5, you should also copy COMMAND.COM file. From version 5 onwards it is transferred automatically when you create a system disk.

Quick formatting

If you have DOS version 5 or higher, you will be able to perform a quick format in a fraction of the time if the disk has already been formatted once before. To format a disk in drive A type:

```
C> format a: /q
```

This is useful if you have disks with old files, that are no longer required and you want to use them for storing new information.

Formatting to a different capacity

Also newly introduced in DOS 5 was the ability to format a disk to a different capacity. For example,

```
C> format a: /f:720
```

will format 720K disks in a 3½" 1.44MB drive.

```
C> format a: /f:360
```

will format 360K disks in a 5¼" 1.2MB drive.

This is useful if you want to copy files for someone who only has a lower capacity drive.

You cannot format a disk to a higher capacity than your drive and you should not format a higher density disk to a lower one either.

Most of the time of course, DOS will automatically format disks according to the type of drive you have. Also remember that the different capacity options in the format command shown above, will only work if you have DOS version 5 or higher.

Duliplicating disks

If you want to make an exact copy of a floppy disk, copying all files, the DISKCOPY command is probably the best one to use. It is ideal for making copies of software master disks you have purchased.

The two disks must be of the same type and capacity before you can use the DISKCOPY command.

If the the target disk is not formatted, it does not matter because it will be formatted in the same operation.

To duplicate a disk from drive A (source) to a disk inserted in drive B (target), type:

```
C> diskcopy a: b:
```

If you only have one disk drive and you want to duplicate a disk, type:

```
C> diskcopy a: a:
```

You'll be asked to insert the source disk and then the target disk. Sometimes if there is a lot of information to transfer you may be asked to swap the source and target disks several times. Just follow the instructions DOS gives you and ensure that the disks are labelled properly so that you insert the correct ones.

Write-protect the source disk (read the section earlier in this chapter to remind yourself how to write-protect disks) to ensure that you don't accidently use it as the target disk and overwrite the original information to be copied.

Comparing disks

If you want to compare the contents of two disks sometime after the DISKCOPY operation, use the DISKCOMP command:

```
C> diskcomp a: b:
```

The above command will compare disks inserted in drive A and B to ensure that they are identical.

If you have DOS 5 or a higher version you can use the verify switch in the DISKCOPY command to compare the disks after the duplication in the same operation:

```
C> diskcopy a: b: /v
```

You cannot use the DISKCOMP command after using the COPY command to transfer all files from one disk to another. This is because files may have been copied to different tracks on the disk and so the contents are not guaranteed to match exactly.

CHAPTER 7

Hard Disk
for Storage

In this chapter you will learn ....

➤ About formatting a hard disk

➤ About checking your hard disk

➤ About freeing hard disk space

➤ About defragmenting your hard disk

➤ About compressing and scanning your hard disk

A hard disk is similar to a floppy disk. It is a magnetic coated medium spinning at high speeds, whilst the read/ write head moves between its concentric circles (or tracks). The difference between a floppy disk and a hard disk is that a hard disk spins much faster, contains several magnetic coated platters which are more rigid, and it is enclosed in a metal casing for protection. The differences allow hard disks to offer much more storage and they also provide a much faster response time.

Formatting a hard disk

Most PC suppliers provide you with the hard disk already formatted. You should not usually have to perform this task yourself - unless you experience a major corruption of the hard disk, or if you have purchased a new hard disk.

The basic procedure for formatting a hard disk is the same as formatting a floppy disk (using the FORMAT command described in the previous chapter). However, it will take much longer because there is more to format.

Be careful that you don't accidently format your hard disk instead of a floppy disk (by typing FORMAT C:). You will loose important information. DOS will just issue this warning message before it wipes off your whole hard disk:

```
WARNING, ALL DATA ON NON-REMOVABLE DISK
DRIVE C: WILL BE LOST!
Proceed with Format (Y/N)?
```

Check disk

It is good practice to check the status of files and directories on your hard disk regularly. You will need to do this anyway before installing new software to your hard disk to ensure that there is enough space.

The CHKDSK command is usually used to check the hard disk, although you can use it to check your floppy disks too. To issue the command, just type:

```
C> chkdsk
```

DOS will then display something like the following:

```
Volume Serial Number is 1ABA-725A
Errors found, F parameter not specified
Corrections will not be written to disk


    415 lost allocation units found in 6 chains.
    1699840 bytes disk space would be freed

 244801536 bytes total disk space
   2244608 bytes in 7 hidden files
    573440 bytes in 128 directories
 217489408 bytes in 3723 user files
  22794240 bytes available on disk

      4096 bytes in each allocation unit
     59766 total allocation units on disk
      5565 available allocation units on disk

    655360 total bytes memory
    598960 bytes free
```

You'll notice that as well as statistics on files, directories, disk space and memory, the second line states 'Errors found, F parameter not specified'. Don't worry! You'll get this when portions of some files have been separated from their original files. These are called "lost clusters". Usually they are of no use and you should convert these clusters to files and then delete the files to save space on the disk. To achieve this, first issue the CHKDSK command again, but this time with the 'F' parameter (F stands for Fix if you want to know) as instructed by DOS:

```
C> chkdsk /f
```

This will find the lost clusters and convert them to sequentially numbered files with .chk extensions e.g. file0000.chk, file0001.chk, file0003.chk, etc. They will be written to your root directory and to delete them all just type:

```
C> del file*.chk
```

Before using the CHKDSK /F, exit from any applications running, otherwise you may lose data. You should even exit from Windows and the MS-DOS shell, if they are active.

Defragmenter

A file is not always stored on your hard disk in a single contiguous place. It may be split and stored in different areas of the hard disk, particularly if you are frequently updating and deleting your files. This fragmentation doesn't damage the files, but when you want to access them it can be quite a long process as DOS hunts down all the parts.

If you have DOS version 6.0 or later, you'll be able to reorganise your disk so that each file stored (perhaps as several pieces scattered all over the disk) is read and then written back in continuous storage locations. This will speed up access to all your files when you need to use them again. This procedure is called *defragmentation*. It involves first issuing the CHKDSK command with the /F parameter as already discussed.

Next, type the following command:

```
C> defrag
```

A list of the drives on your computer will be displayed and you can use the Up Arrow and Down Arrow keys to move to the drive you wish to defragment and then press Enter. The defragmenter looks at your disk and recommends a way to do the defragmentation. Press Enter and the defragmentation process will occur.

Note that this may take some time depending on the size and the number of files stored. A map of the disk will be displayed and it will be reassuring to see blocks of files being sorted.

Disk compression

If you have DOS version 6.0 or 6.2 you will be able to run DoubleSpace to approximately double your hard disk space or at least increase it by one and a half times.

Microsoft, however, were found to have infringed Stac Electronic's compression technology in DoubleSpace by the U.S. courts. As well as paying a big fine to Stac, Microsoft had to recall versions with DoubleSpace from their resellers in the U.S. and replace it with a special version without the impeding technology. Microsoft also quickly followed with a special version, DOS 6.22, which uses DriveSpace instead. Functionally they are the same, but DriveSpace doesn't infringe Stac's patent. After all of this, Microsoft and Stac reached an agreement so that Microsoft can continue to use DoubleSpace and sell MS-DOS 6.2 worldwide. Now lets take a closer look at DoubleSpace.

You can use compression to increase space on a floppy disk, but it's normally used on your 'C' hard disk.

To set up DoubleSpace, type:

```
C> dblspace
```

After the Welcome screen you'll be prompted to choose between Express and Custom setup. Choose Express unless you have the technical know-how about DoubleSpace.

As part of this routine, DoubleSpace will initially scan your disk and defragment it. It will also restart your computer just before starting to compress your disk. Then it will display:

```
DoubleSpace is now compressing drive C.
Start time:              17:03:18
Current time:            17:08:26
Estimated finish time:   18:44
Time left:               About 1 hour and 38 minutes

Currently compressing C:\WINDOWS\SYSTEM\
```

A status bar at the bottom also shows the percentage of compression already completed. You'll also notice that the Estimated finish time and Time left figures will be re-adjusted as the compression progresses and DoubleSpace is able to make a more and more accurate estimate - don't be surprised if in the early stages you see the time left increase occassionally instead of going down.

The amount of time taken will vary for everyone. It depends on the amount of information on the disk that needs to be compressed and the speed of your computer.

During the compression, DoubleSpace will need to restart your computer again.

Once it's over, DoubleSpace will display:

```
DoubleSpace has finished compressing drive C.

 Free space before compression:4.5MB
 Free space after compression: 169.7 MB
 Compression ratio:            2.5 to 1
 Total time to compress:       1 hour and 31 minutes

DoubleSpace has created a new drive H that contains
29.4 MB of uncompressed space, 2.0 MB of which will
be used by Microsoft Windows. The remainder of this
space has been set aside for files that must remain
uncompressed.

To exit from DoubleSpace and restart your computer,
press ENTER.
```

Do not alter or remove the files in the new drive created by DoubleSpace (in our example it's drive H). These are important system files that cannot be compressed and therefore had to be separated from your main disk drive (C).

Scanning your hard disk

A new utility, called SCANDISK, allows you to analyse and repair problems with your disk. It can be used on your main hard disk, whether it's DoubleSpace compressed or not, or any other disk. To start it, type:

```
C> scandisk c:
```

to scan your C hard disk. The program will start to analyse and check the directory structure stored on the disk, the File Allocation Table (or FAT), the rest of the file system and then, it will ask you if you want to perform a surface scan because this takes a little longer.

A surface scan checks each cluster on disk to ensure that data can be read and written. If the disk being scanned is DoubleSpace compressed, it will also check that data can be decompressed from it. It is recommended that you perform a surface scan on your important disk frequently.

If an error is found during scandisk, a dialog box will be displayed and the error explained. A Fix It button option may be used to remedy the problem.

CHAPTER

8

Understanding Directories

In this chapter you will learn ....

> What a multi-level directory structure is

> What a pathname is

> How to expand a directory tree

> How to create, change and delete directories

> How to delete a whole directory tree

Hard disks offer much greater storage capability than floppies, as discussed in the previous chapter. It is not uncommon to find hard disks with several hundred megabytes of storage. However, most computers nowadays offer a minimum of around 100-200 megabytes of hard disk already built into the system unit as standard.

The problem with so much storage is that it is easy to populate it with so many files that it becomes difficult to find anything. To resolve this problem, DOS provides us with a *multi-level directory structure*.

This chapter is all about how to nagivate within the multi-level directory and use it more effectively. Commands described here also apply to floppy disks, however it is more common to use them to keep your hard disk organised, as there is usually much more information stored here.

What exactly is a multi-level directory structure?

A multi-level directory structure allows a convenient way of keeping related files or information together in a hierarchy of directories.

It is sometimes referred to as an 'upside-down tree'. The root directory is at the top. This is created automatically when you format a disk. You can store files here or create other directories from the root, called sub-directories. Within each sub-directory you can store more files or create further sub-directories. The tree therefore, can be expanded and structured in the way you want to keep your information organised.

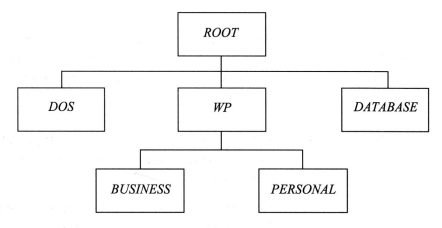

For example, if you have bought a wordprocessor, create a WP directory to store all its program files. Then within this directory, create a sub-directory BUSINESS to store all your business communication and another sub-directory PERSONAL to store all your personal letters, as shown.

Most software products can automatically create their own directories when you install them. However, you still need to create sub-directories within these to organise your data.

What are pathnames?

The concept of pathnames is important in a multi-level directory. A pathname is the route DOS needs to know to find a file. For example, if you have a file called LETTER1.DOC in the PERSONAL sub-directory, the pathname is:

```
C:\wp\personal
```

You need to specify the path by giving DOS all the sub-directory names from the root, in the correct order, to get to the file. You could have another file, also called LETTER1.DOC in the BUSINESS sub-directory. However, DOS will always access the correct file because the pathname will be different.

Most DOS commands should have the pathname joined with the filename. So for example, if you want to copy the file LET1.DOC to the root directory, type:

```
A> copy c:\wp\personal\let1.doc c:\
```

You can specify just the filename if you are already in the appropriate directory or if you have previously issued a PATH command.

The path command establishes a link to one or more directories that are accessed regularly - thus avoiding the need to type the path all the time. A good example of this is establishing a path to the DOS directory itself. Many external commands, like FORMAT, UNDELETE and so on, are program files stored in the DOS directory instead of residing in memory. Therefore, to use them without having to type the path all the time, just type the path command once:

```
C> path c:\dos
```

This statement usually exists in the AUTOEXEC.BAT file (see later). This way you do not need to type it every time after powering on.

Directory tree

The concept of pathnames is fine, except how do you find the exact path or all the levels of sub-directories linked together? From the shell it is easy because you can expand any directory branch by clicking on its folder icons - all sub-directories belonging to it will be indented and displayed under it.

However, if you don't have the shell installed or don't like using it, there is a way of displaying the directory tree from the DOS command prompt. Just type TREE from any directory to see all levels of sub-directories that belong to it.

```
C> tree
```

HANDY TIP

If you type the tree command from the root or another directory that has many levels of sub-directories, you may not see all of them as they will scroll off the screen. Therefore type:

```
C> tree|more
```

Now the display will pause for you to press "any key" when a screen-full of the directory tree is displayed.

Here is an example of the type of display you can expect from a directory tree:

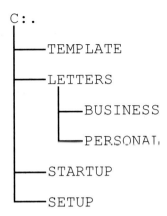

```
C:.
    ├────TEMPLATE
    ├────LETTERS
    │        ├────BUSINESS
    │        └────PERSONAL
    ├─────STARTUP
    └─────SETUP
```

Using 'Deltree'

If you are using DOS version 6.0 or higher there is a new powerful command called DELTREE. It deletes the specified directory and everything under it in one fell swoop - that is all the files and any sub-directories (and files within them). An entire directory tree will disappear with this one simple command. To use it type:

```
C> deltree wp
```

This command will delete all the files in the wp directory, all the files in all the sub-directories from wp, the sub-directories themselves and the wp directory.

Although a Y/N confirmation prompt is displayed before the tree is deleted make sure you think twice before issuing this command. Use the tree command first to display all the directories that will be deleted.

```
C> deltree \
```

will delete everything on your hard disk.

Creating directories

If you want to create a new directory, you need to first go to the directory from which you want to create a new sub-directory (see Changing directories). This is called the 'parent' directory of the one you are going to create. Also, and quite logically, your new directory will be a 'child' to the parent directory. To create a new directory type:

```
C> md dir
```

where md is short for Make Directory (you can type mkdir instead) and 'dir' is the name you want to give to the new directory.

Changing directories

When you create a new directory, DOS does not automatically make it the current directory. You have to issue the Change Directory command to access it:

```
C> cd dir
```

where cd is short for Change Directory (you can type chdir instead). The 'dir' above can be just the directory name for the next level or a path to the ultimate directory you want to change to. For example, you can type:

```
C> cd wp\business
```

If you want to move up to the wp directory from business, type:

```
C> cd ..
```

HANDY TIP

You will see a dot-dot (or two dots) and dot (single dot) files created automatically when you create a new directory. The two dots represent the parent directory of the current directory and the single dot on its own represents the current directory itself.

REMEMBER

To move straight up to the root directory from anywhere, type:

```
C> cd \
```

Removing directories

You cannot usually remove or delete a directory if it contains any files. Therefore, before trying to remove a directory, make sure that you have first deleted all the files within it. Then type:

```
C> rd dir
```

where rd is short for Remove Directory (you can type rmdir instead).

CHAPTER 9

Some more
on Files

In this chapter you will learn ....

➢ About the common naming conventions for DOS files

➢ About displaying and changing file attributes

➢ About sorting files in a different order

➢ How to find lost files

➢ The benefits of using XCOPY instead of the COPY command

This chapter builds on basic file management you learned in Chapter 4. You'll remember that files are basic units of information stored on disk and managed by DOS. One way to organise files is by creating suitable directories (as discussed in the last chapter) and storing them in the appropriate directory so that they'll be easy to find and work with. Another is to use sensible naming conventions so that it is obvious what information a particular file contains just from it's name.

Naming conventions

When creating DOS files, either from your software applications like Microsoft Word, Excel or WordPerfect, or by using the DOS Editor (see later), you must follow certain rules for naming them.

A DOS filename consists of a name and an extension (sometimes called the *filetype*). You can use a maximum of eight characters for the name and three characters for the extension, separated by a period. Most software applications will automatically create the extension part of the full name so that it is possible to distinguish which applications were used to create the files. For example, Word uses .DOC, Excel uses .XLS, and so on.

Common file types that DOS uses are:

.EXE (executable) or **.COM** (command)
These files contain programs that are executed or run.

.SYS (system)
These files contain information about your system. Usually they describe characteristics of components you can connect to your PC. These are called device drivers.

.BAT (batch)
These files contain a list of commands that DOS will execute sequentially.

It does not matter whether you use uppercase or lowercase letters in the file type or any part of the file name. DOS treats them as being the same.

You can use any letters of the alphabet, numbers and the following special characters to name a file:

_	underscore	&	ampersand
^	caret	-	hyphen
$	dollar	{}	braces
~	tilde	()	parenthesis
!	exclamation	@	at symbol
#	number symbol	'	apostrophe
%	percent	`	grave accent

No other characters are valid in the file name. In naming your files, however, it is best to try and avoid using the characters above if you can. You should adopt a simple naming convention for all your files so that you can find any file easily. For example:

HK130594.DOC *This is a word document. It was a letter written on 13th May 1994 to a person with initials HK.*

If two letters are not enough to identify who the communication was made to, then adopt six letters and reserve two letters for a sequential number so that the most recent communication will be the highest number. e.g.

COMPST01.DOC *Here 3 letters were written to*
COMPST02.DOC *Computer Step COMPST03.DOC*
COMPST03.DOC *being the latest one.*

HANDY TIP

You'll still be able to find out the exact date these letters were created from the directory listings of the files.

Changing file attributes

There are several attributes or characteristics a file possesses. These include the size of the file, date of creation, and time of creation - all updated by the system automatically and can be displayed on a directory listing of files. However, there are other attributes which you can define and control.

To display these attributes, type

```
C> attrib filename
```

where *filename* can be a name of one file or a wildcard can be used (e.g. *.*) to display attributes of several files. An example of the output from this command may look something like:

```
A    SHR C:\IO.SYS
A    SHR C:\MSDOS.SYS
A      R C:\COMMAND.COM
A        C:\AUTOEXEC.BAT
```

The four files listed above are all prefixed with one or more of the following attributes:

A (for Archive). Indicates whether a file has changed since it was last backed up.

S (for System). System files are not seen in the file or directory listing. You should not use this attribute. It is reserved for DOS system files only.

H (for Hidden). Hidden files are also not seen in the file or directory listing. You can use this attribute if you have a secret file you do not want anyone else to see.

R (for Read only). These files cannot be changed. You can only read or display them.

To change attributes, use the ATTRIB command again, but this time prefix the attribute that needs to be changed with '+' to select it or '-' to deselect it. For example:

```
C> attrib   +h   secret.doc
C> attrib   -h  +r   secret.doc
C> attrib   -a   -s   -h   -r   msdos.sys
```

Sorting files

Files can be sorted in various ways by using /o switch or option in the DIR command. You have a choice of sorting files in one of the following order:

/on	file name alphabetically
/o-n	file name alphabctically, but descending
/oe	extension (file type) alphabetically
/o-e	extension alphabetically, but descending
/od	date increasing (oldest file first)
/o-d	date decreasing (newest file first)
/os	file size increasing (smallest file first)
/o-s	file size decreasing (largest file first)

You can combine options in the DIR command. For example:

```
C> dir /od /p
```

to display files from the current directory, starting with the oldest and pausing after a screen full.

Finding a lost file

By creating meaningful directory names and also devising sensible naming conventions for files as discussed earlier in this chapter, it will not be difficult to find a particular file.

However, if you're still having problems and you have too many directories and files to look through to find your file, there is a quicker way. Type:

```
C> dir \lostfile.doc /s
```

where lostfile.doc is the name of the file you are looking for. After you press the Enter key your computer may take a little time to look through the whole disk for your file and if the file is found, it will display the details:

```
Directory of C:\WINWORD\STRANGE
LOSTFILE   DOC  13,824  16/05/94 10:06
    1 file(s)        13,824 bytes
```

To access the file, use the CD command to go to the directory path displayed above.

If more than one copy of the file exists in different directories then all occurrences of the file and it's respective directory will be displayed.

If you still cannot find your file then you've probably called it something else or saved it on another disk. Wild cards may help if you can only remember part of the name. For example, LOST*.DOC or ????FILE.DOC.

Using the eXtended Copy (XCOPY) command

The COPY command can be used to copy individual files, groups of files or directories, and it has already been discussed in Chapter 4.

The XCOPY command is very similar to the COPY command and can be thought of as an eXtended version it. You can use it in the same way as the COPY command, but there are additional options available. Perhaps the best way to illustrate its capabilities is with a few examples:

```
C> xcopy c:\wp a: /s /e
```

/s option will also copy all sub-directories under wp, but not if the sub-directories are empty. /e will ensure that even empty sub-directories are copied so that the original tree structure is maintained completely.

```
C> xcopy c:\wp a: d:31-12-93
```

only copies files that were changed on or after 31st of December 1993.

```
C> xcopy a: c:\newprogs
```

will copy all files from the 'a' disk to newprogs directory in drive 'c'. The unique feature is that even if newprogs directory does not exist, XCOPY will create it first automatically before copying the files.

```
C> xcopy c:\wp a: /m
```

will only copy files to 'a' if they have been modified since the last BACKUP or XCOPY operation. The files are also tagged so that next time they will not be overwritten unless they are different. Use the /a option with XCOPY next time to only copy changed files.

SECTION THREE

Important
Techniques
and Procedures

Apart from storing and manipulating files you will also need to work with software or programs. You'll learn all about this here and also how to use DOS programs and other DOS commands from the Windows environment if that is what you normally use. Some of the more advanced features will also be covered in a friendly way, including special redirectional commands, updating the two most important system files that DOS uses and commands that will help you to manage your computer's memory more effectively. Finally, the important subject of security is covered with reference to backups, anti-virus and undeleting files.

Installing and Running Programs

In this chapter you will learn ....

➤ How to install programs

➤ How to get the information out of a README file

➤ How to set up and use programs in the DOS shell

➤ The different ways to run programs

M any of the things you will want to do with your computer will involve the use of commercial software. Some of this may come pre-installed when you buy your computer, but it is likely that you will, at some time, want to install some more software. This chapter shows you how to do this.

Installing software

Commercial software comes on one or (usually) more floppy disks. The information on these disks needs to be transferred onto your hard disk so that you can run the software directly. Often, due to the size of the program, the information that makes up the program may have been compressed using clever mathematical techniques (which you do not need to know). These "compressed" files must be "decompressed" before the computer can understand the information they contain. This is done by a program which will be on one of the installation disks. The decompressor program will be loaded into your computer first. It will then read in the information from the disks and decompress it.

The installation of software is usually a painless process. You should refer to the manual which comes with the software before installing, to ensure that you understand the procedure which may vary slightly from the one described here.

One thing which is important to remember before you start to install software is that you should have a backup copy of the floppy disks it comes on. This is a safety precaution in case both the versions on your hard disk and the original floppy disks are damaged or erased.

To install a piece of DOS-based software, you will insert the first disk, change to the correct disk drive and type the name of the install program, which is usually SETUP or INSTALL. This will start the install routine, and you will usually see a screen which will allow you to choose how the program is installed. You'll also see prompts, telling you when to insert the next disk.

If you are installing a Windows program, first insert the SETUP floppy disk into the A disk drive. Then in Windows, select Run from the File menu in Program Manager. In the command line box type:

```
a:\setup
```

Type SETUP or whatever the installation program is called (sometimes it is called INSTALL). Then click on OK and the installation will start, prompting you to select features you want to install and displaying the progress.

Things you may need to do during installation

You will often be asked to decide which directory the program should be installed into. You will usually be given a dcfault choice by the setup program and it is usually better to choose this directory. If you want to use another directory to store the program in just type the directory name.

You may be asked by the installation screens to provide information about your system, such as the type of graphics adapter that you have. It is thus a good idea to have the manual for your computer handy when you install software. More sophisticated software is often able to determine the information about your system that it needs to know without your help.

You shouldn't worry if, when you install the software, you don't use all the disks which came with the package. Not all the software may need to be installed. This is certainly the case if you chose to install only some of the components of your package in the first place. Also if you are upgrading your software from an earlier version, it may not always be necessary to copy all the files as some of them may have remained unchanged from an earlier version.

When a software package runs it may need certain parts of your system to work in a particular way. If this is the case your AUTOEXEC.BAT and/or CONFIG.SYS files (which control how your system operates) may need altering. Many software packages will make these alterations for you, but others may need you to do them yourself. If this is the case the manual will tell you the instructions which need to be added to these files. See Chapter 13 for details of how to modify these files.

Installing large programs

Many current software packages, particularly wordprocessors, graphics packages and DTP packages are very large, requiring space that you may not have on your hard disk.

You can often customise the installation of these programs and choose not to install features you don't strictly need, thus saving space on your hard disk. If you are installing a word processor, for example, you might choose not to install the package's Thesaurus or foreign language facilities, if you're not going to need them.

README files

Most software packages come with a file called README (or some variant on this name). This file contains information about the package which is likely to be of use to you. In particular, it may contain information about any changes which have been made to the software after the manual was written. This sometimes occurs when there are last minute changes to the package (perhaps to iron-out some minor fault).

It is important to look at the README file before you use the software and it is often a good idea to look at it even before you install the package.

To access the README file, look at the file extension. This is likely to be .TXT or .WRI which is common for Windows programs. If it is a .TXT file, type the following at the command prompt.

```
C> type readme.txt | more
```

This will print the file out a screenful at a time, with the word MORE written at the bottom of the screen. To move onto the next screen simply press any key. The MORE command is described in Chapter 12. If you want to have a permanent copy of the README file, type the following at the command prompt:

```
C> type readme.txt > prn
```

This will print the README file to your printer.

If you have Windows, double-click with the mouse on the Write icon in the Accessories group to start Write, which is a simple word processor program. Then select Open from the File drop-down menu and type the name README.WRI (or .TXT) in the File Name box. Click on OK and the README file will be displayed. If you want a permanent copy of the file printed, then select print from the file menu and click on OK. If you have another Windows word processor, you can use it in the same way to display a .TXT file.

Using programs in the DOS Shell

If you have installed the DOS shell, you will see some programs already set up in the Main area of the shell. These are Command Prompt, Disk Utilities, Editor and MS-DOS QBasic.

Some of these are program groups like Disk Utilities. Others are program items. If you select a group you will not run any program, but another menu with a further selection of programs will be displayed.

You can add your own program groups and items to the standard ones provided. If you are going to be using a particular program frequently, like Windows or a word processor, it is worthwhile setting it up in the Main area.

Setting up Program Groups and Items

To set up a new program group or item, select New from the File menu. You will only see this option if the Main area is highlighted or selected first. Also ensure that you have displayed the group you want to add your program group or item to. Once you have selected New, you will be presented with a New Program Object dialog box as shown below:

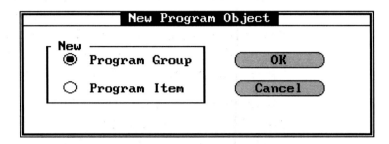

Choose Program Group or Item from the dialog box and then OK. If you choose Program Group, you will get another simple dialog box - Add Group:

```
┌──────────────────────── Add Group ────────────────────────┐
│                                                            │
│   Required                                                 │
│                                                            │
│     Title . . . .          [_                    ]         │
│                                                            │
│   Optional                                                 │
│                                                            │
│     Help Text . .          [                     ]         │
│                                                            │
│     Password  . .          [              ]               │
│                                                            │
│                                                            │
│       ( OK )          ( Cancel )          ( Help )         │
│                                                            │
└────────────────────────────────────────────────────────────┘
```

Type in the Title you want to give your group. Whatever text you type here will be displayed in the shell. You can also type a help message and a password if you want to. The password will stop unauthorised people using your application. This

BEWARE

security check is only available via the shell, though. Anyone can run your programs from the command prompt. Choose OK and you will see the group title appear in the Main program list.

If, at a later date, you want to change the title of your group or the help text and password, you can do so by choosing Properties from the File menu. In order to change the password, you will need to provide the current password. Otherwise, of course, there is no security!

Choose Properties also, to alter the details for a program item. To add a program item initially, select New from the File menu (as you did for a group). Then choose Program Item from the dialog box to get the Add Program dialog box as shown below:

```
┌─────────────────────────────────────────────────────────┐
│                        ▐ Add Program ▌                    │
│ ┌───────────────────────────────────────────────────────┐│
│                                                           │
│   Program Title . . . .  [_                            ]  │
│                                                           │
│   Commands  . . . . . .  [                             ]  │
│                                                           │
│   Startup Directory . .  [                             ]  │
│                                                           │
│   Application Shortcut Key       [                     ]  │
│                                                           │
│   [X] Pause after exit        Password . .  [          ]  │
│       ( OK )    ( Cancel )    ( Help )   ( Advanced... )   │
│ └───────────────────────────────────────────────────────┘│
└─────────────────────────────────────────────────────────┘
```

Type in the Title as you did for a group. It will again be displayed in the shell and used by you to identify and run the program. In the Commands box, type the exact command to start the program (e.g. WORD, WP, EXCEL, 123). You can often follow the command with a filename that you want loaded as soon as you go into that program. e.g. For a file in WORD type C:\WINWORD\BUSINESS\CUST9412.DOC.

If you do not always want to work with a particular file, but there are many files that you access frequently from a particular directory, then type the path for that directory in the Startup Directory box. You will automatically access this directory as soon as the program has started. e.g. C:\WINWORD\BUSINESS.

The Application Shortcut Key enables you to switch to this program instantly once it has been started in the Active task list (see Task Swapper later). The shortcut key has to be an 'Alt', 'Ctrl' or 'Shift' key combination. You cannot use a combination like Alt+F, because the shell uses it to display the File menu. You can include this shortcut key as part of your title, so that it's displayed and you will not have to remember it.

To be able to return to the shell after you exit the program, you need to keep the Pause after exit box selected. The password to the right of it is optional. If you type one in, you will be required to type it in every time before you can run the program. Choose OK to confirm your settings and to set up the new program item.

Working with Program Groups and Items

Remember that you can set up as many programs as you want. You can set up the same program with different filenames or directories. Your actual programs are not duplicated - they are just accessed from the shell in different ways. You can also delete program groups or items by choosing Delete from the File menu after highlighting the relevant program. Your actual programs will not be deleted - only the entries in the shell to access them easily, will be deleted.

It is possible to rearrange program group or item entries, once they have been created. Highlight the entry you want to move. Then, choose Reorder from the File menu. Nothing will happen. But if you select a location and double-click there or press the Enter key, your intial entry will move there. You can use this procedure to reorder your program entries alphabetically, or put the most frequently used programs at the top.

Starting programs from Windows

In Windows you select the group icon where the program is stored and double-click on the program icon. Alternatively, select Run from the File menu, type in the name of the .EXE or .COM file in the command line box and click on OK. In File Manager you can double-click on a .EXE or .COM file to start it. You can set up DOS programs in Windows so that they can be run by double-clicking on an icon - for more details see Chapter 11.

Starting programs from the DOS Shell

There are several ways of starting or running programs from the shell. If you have gone to the trouble of setting up programs in the program list as described, the easiest way to start a program is to just double-click on its title with the mouse. Using the keyboard, you can highlight the program you want with the arrow keys and then press Enter. If you have set up program groups, selecting them will display other groups or program items that you can run.

You can also double-click a program file from the File list to run it. They usually have an extension of .EXE or .COM. Another useful technique is to select a file you want to use with your program by highlighting it with the mouse and then drag it keeping the left mouse button depressed, to a program file, either in the File list or Program list. Let go of the file icon once it's on the program file. Your program will then start and use the file you just dropped on it.

Another way to start a program is to just select Run from the File menu and type in the name of the program you want to run. You may also need to type the path to the program if it does not exist in the AUTOEXEC.BAT file (see Chapter 13).

```
┌──────────────────────── Run ────────────────────────┐
│                                                      │
│  Command Line . .   [                              ] │
│                                                      │
│         (    OK    )         (  Cancel  )            │
│                                                      │
└──────────────────────────────────────────────────────┘
```

Starting programs from the Command Prompt

Instead of typing the command to run your program from the shell, you can choose Command Prompt from the Main program group, or press Shift+F9, to temporarily go to the DOS command prompt.

From the command prompt type the name of the program you want to run or execute:

```
C> word
```

The above, for example, will run the Microsoft Word program. There should be a WORD.EXE file on your disk, but you do not need to type the .EXE extension to run the program.

If the program is not in the current directory, you need to also type the path to the directory or have it established prior to issuing the command (as discussed before).

To go back to the shell, type:

```
C> exit
```

REMEMBER

If you want to remove the shell completely from memory and go to the command prompt permanently, choose Exit from the File menu or press F3 or Alt+F4.

Once you are at the command prompt, you can of course, do more than just run programs. You can issue any number of DOS commands to perform tasks that are easier to achieve from the command prompt.

Task Swapper

The task swapper is a relatively new facility first introduced in version 5 of the DOS shell. It enables you to start and run several programs simultaneously and switch between them almost instantly.

To activate the task swapper, choose it from the Options menu. An Active Task list is created to the right of the main program group. You can add several programs to this list. Just select the programs from the program list of the file list as you normally do run them (double-click with the mouse or highlight with arrow keys and press Enter), except have the Shift key pressed too. This will not run the programs straight away, but will add the program entries to the active task list.

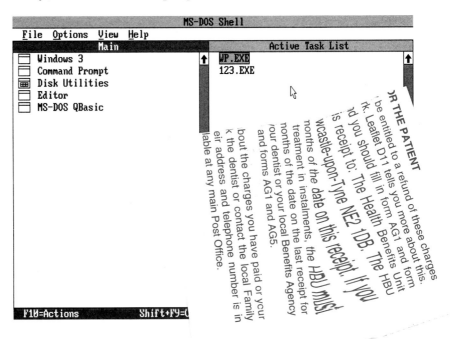

You can start programs from the active task list by double-clicking with the mouse or highlighting an entry with arrow keys and pressing Enter. Once you are running a program, say a word processor, and have submitted a print of a long document from it, you can switch to say your spreadsheet, first by pressing Ctrl+Esc from the word processor to get back to the shell. Then, press the Alt+Tab keys until the spreadsheet program appears. Let go of the Alt key to select it.

If you run Windows from the DOS 5 (or later) shell, you will not be able to use Ctrl+Esc to switch back to the shell. This is because Windows also uses Ctrl+Esc key combination to activate its own task list. Therefore, you will have to exit Windows to return to the shell.

Also if you run memory-resident utilities, also known as TSR (Terminate and Stay Resident) programs, from the shell, you may find that the display is not cleared when you return to the shell. To display the shell properly again, choose Repaint Screen from the View menu or press Shift+F5.

Choose Refresh from the View menu or press F5 if you return to the shell from an application, like a word processor, that creates new files or deletes them. The File list and the Directory tree displays will then be updated in the shell.

Using DOS
from Windows

In this chapter you will learn ....

➤ How to access the DOS command prompt from Windows

➤ How to set up DOS programs to run from Windows

➤ About DOS functions you shouldn't use from Windows

■ ■

I f you have Windows you can access DOS facilities without having to exit from Windows. In this chapter you will be shown what you can and can't do from Windows.

Accessing the DOS Command Prompt

To gain access to the DOS command prompt from Windows, double click on the MS-DOS prompt icon in the Main group. You will be transferred to the command prompt, with the Windows directory selected. You can issue DOS commands from here as usual. There are two ways the command prompt can appear: full screen or inside a window. To change from one display format to another press Alt+Enter. You can use Alt+Tab to switch from the command prompt to another window. If you have the command prompt as a window it can be used in the standard way and can be minimised, moved, resized etc.

When you want to stop using DOS, type EXIT and press Enter and you will be returned to Windows. This will work both from the full screen and windowed display.

What you shouldn't do from Windows

There are some DOS commands which should not be issued from the command prompt when you are still running Windows. These are:

```
chkdsk /f
append
dblspace
defrag
emm386
fastopen
memmaker
mscdex
nlsfunc
smartdrv
subst
vsafe
```

You should not use these commands because they may affect files which are vital to the operation of Windows. If you want to use any of these commands, first exit from Windows and then type the commands at the command prompt.

You can't use the DOSShell if you have the Windowed rather than the full-screen display.

Setting up DOS programs to work from Windows

You may want to use a DOS-based program directly from the Windows interface without having to go to the command prompt. This can be done by setting up the program so that it can run within the Windows environment. You can set it up so that it will have an icon which can be double-clicked to give access to the program.

To set up a DOS program, double-click on the PIF Editor icon in the Main group. The PIF Editor dialog box is then displayed. In this dialog box you should fill in the name of the program. Then fill in a title for the program that will appear under the icon in the Window. Type the path and directory where the program file is found. Ensure that there is a bullet in the circle next to Windowed in the Display usage section. Now click on Save As from the File drop-down menu and a dialog box will appear. Type a filename for your DOS program with an extension of PIF and click on OK. Choose Exit from the File menu to leave the PIF Editor screen.

Ensure that the group that you want to create the program item into is selected by clicking on it. Now select New from the Program Manager File menu. Click on Program Item option if it is not already selected. Click on OK and fill in a description of the program. In the command line box, type the path and name of the PIF file you saved and click on OK. The program item will be created in your selected group, with an MS-DOS icon and the name you gave the program in the Program item dialog box.

You can now double-click on the icon to start the application and use it as normal without exiting from Windows.

CHAPTER

12

Special Commands for Redirecting Information

In this chapter you will learn ....

➤ About general redirection of input and output

➤ How to use Filters to sort information

➤ How to use Pipes to send information between DOS commands

■ ■

This Chapter is about redirectional commands in DOS. These are usually regarded as advanced commands and therefore are not available from the shell. However, these are not really that difficult, as you will learn. Redirectional commands are generally issued from the command prompt.

Basic Redirection

Normally, you issue DOS commands from the keyboard. The keyboard is also called an input console, or CON, as far as DOS is concerned. The output from the command is displayed on your monitor (or output console, but again just CON to DOS). Redirection is all about changing this norm.

For example, the output of the DIR command can be redirected to the printer instead of the screen by:

```
C> dir > prn
```

The > (greater-than) symbol is used for redirection. Make sure that the printer is ON before you issue this command.

You can even redirect the directory list to a file by:

```
C> dir > myfiles.txt
```

The file will be created automatically if it does not exist. If it does exist, the information in it will be over-written with the latest directory list. To avoid this use >> (two greater- than) symbols:

```
C> dir >> myfiles.txt
```

New information will now be added to whatever was in the file, rather than replacing it.

If you want to use your printer as a typewriter and print text on it as you are typing, redirect your input console directly to the printer:

```
C> copy con prn
```

After issuing this command, everything you type will echo to the screen and also get printed straightaway. To finish, press F6 followed by the Enter key.

You could also print a file, using the COPY command rather than the print command:

```
C> copy custlist.txt prn
```

You can use LPT1 instead of PRN to address your first printer, but this command may not work with all laser printers.

Apart from these basic redirection commands, there are two groups of redirectional commands known as filters and pipes.

Filters

We can use the analogy of the water system to understand filter commands. If you want to purify water in a pipe, you would use a filter to eliminate undesired substances or to extract clean water. Similarly, DOS uses filter commands to modify or select information, as required. The main filter commands are SORT, FIND and MORE.

The SORT command sorts a file alphabetically, thereby changing it (or filtering it). FIND can look for certain text in files. It will only output lines from a file that match the text. MORE is a little less obvious. It ensures that output from a command or file is displayed a page at a time. It puts the word 'MORE' at the bottom of the screen after a screen-full of output is displayed, if there is more to come. You have to press a key to continue the display. It effectively filters the output into screen-fulls and adds 'MORE'.

```
C> more < custlist.txt
```

This will redirect the contents of the file to the screen. Notice that the redirection symbol is pointing in the opposite direction to that described earlier. It always points in the direction the information is flowing.

```
C> find "W1" < custlist.txt
```

Part of the postcode, 'W1', is being searched for in this file.

```
C> sort < custlist.txt
```

The file, custlist.txt, gets sorted alphabetically. Since the output is not redirected, it will be displayed on the monitor. You can send the output to the printer by:

```
C> sort < custlist.txt > prn
```

Pipes

If you want water to flow from one system to another, you can connect a pipe between the two systems to redirect the flow of water. In the same way, the DOS pipe, symbolised by '|' can redirect output from one DOS command to another.

```
C> dir | sort
```

The output from the directory command is piped to the SORT command filter. It is then displayed on the screen because it is not redirected anywhere else.

```
C> type custlist.txt | more
```

The contents of the file is piped to the MORE so that it is displayed a screen at a time.

You can combine several of these commands. For example:

```
C> find "MALE" < cust | find "W1" | sort > prn
```

This finds all male customers from the cust file, feeds the results to the next section, which will only keep those male customers who live in 'W1' postal area. Then, these are all sorted alphabetically and finally printed.

Updating your AUTOEXEC.BAT and CONFIG.SYS Files

In this chapter you will learn ....

➤ What the AUTOEXEC.BAT and CONFIG.SYS files are

➤ How to edit these two files

➤ The correct order for commands in these files

➤ How to use the DOSKEY utility

➤ How to bypass AUTOEXEC.BAT and CONFIG.SYS commands

You can tailor the way DOS works on your system by modifying two important files. These files are called AUTOEXEC.BAT and CONFIG.SYS. Everytime you switch on, or boot your PC, DOS reads these files and executes the DOS commands within them. Both files usually reside in your root directory.

Most of the time you need not worry about these files. New software you install on your computer usually updates them automatically. It is however useful to know a little about these files so that you can make your system easier to use and more efficient.

Altering AUTOEXEC.BAT and CONFIG.SYS

You can change these files by using EDLIN (stands for Line Editor) if you have an older version than DOS 5. This is quite cumbersome to use. You can only edit a line at a time. From DOS 5 onwards, you are able to use a more sophisticated text editor. To activate it, choose Editor from the Main group in the shell.

Type the name of the file you want to alter in the dialog box. The current text from the file will be displayed and you will be able to make any changes here.

To move the cursor in the editor, simply use the arrow keys or the mouse. To delete characters, press the Del key or Backspace. You can add new lines by typing them in, followed by the Enter key. You can also perform cut-and-paste operations from the Edit menu. Finally, to save your changes, choose Save from the File menu.

To use the editor from the command prompt type:

```
C> edit filename
```

Another way to alter your files is to use your word processor, but you have to save the file you have altered as a pure text file or it will not work properly.

Software installation routines that update your AUTOEXEC.BAT automatically will often save your old version as AUTOEXEC.BAK or AUTOEXEC.OLD. Therefore, if you do not like the changes made to your AUTOEXEC.BAT file, you can rename your version back to the original.

Any changes that are made to the AUTOEXEC.BAT file, either by yourself or by software, will not be effective until you Reset or re-power your computer, or if you re-boot by typing the Ctrl+Alt+Del keys.

AUTOEXEC.BAT

This file is AUTOmatically EXECuted when you start your computer - hence it is called AUTOEXEC.BAT. The .BAT extension means that it is a batch file. This is a special type of file where you can group together several DOS commands. When you type just the name of the file (without .BAT) all the commands in the file will be run sequentially.

AUTOEXEC.BAT can look a little different in different machines. Use the TYPE command to display your version.

An example of an AUTOEXEC.BAT file is:

```
@ECHO OFF
PROMPT $P$G
PATH C:\DOS;C:\WINDOWS
KEYB UK,,C:\DOS\KEYBOARD.SYS
C:\DOS\DOSSHELL
```

Commands in AUTOEXEC.BAT

@ECHO OFF. This line tells DOS not to display the commands (echo them) to the screen as they are being executed.

PROMPT PG. As discussed in Chapter 3, the PROMPT command is used to change the DOS command prompt. The PG is the most common parameter used to always display the directory name at the prompt.

PATH. This was also discussed in Chapter 8. You can specify the directories that you are likely to access most frequently here. If a program you want to execute, or a file you want to access, is in one of the directories specified in the PATH command, you will not need to specify the path to access the file each time.

The order in which you specify the directories is important. If you have the same file name in more than one directory, the version that exists in the first directory in the path, will supersede any subsequent ones you may try and access.

KEYB (KEYBOARD.SYS). This is the keyboard driver. It is used to standardise the keyboard to a particular country. For example, the parameter UK, will allow you to type a £, instead of the default # which is the American standard. The keyboard driver does not have to be in the AUTOEXEC.BAT file - it can be specified in the CONFIG.SYS instead.

DOSSHELL. This will automatically load the DOS shell after you power up.

Another useful command to have in your AUTOEXEC.BAT is SET DIRCMD. This defines the way the Directory command will work when you type DIR. For example:

```
set dircmd = /on /p
```

The /on switch will always display the directory list in alphabetical filename sequence and the /p will pause the list whenever a screenful of the directory is displayed.

DOSKEY

If you have DOS 5 or a later version, there is a useful utility you can use called DOSKEY. It allows you to easily re-issue previously used commands. By typing the following line in your AUTOEXEC.BAT file, it is always there in memory for you to use:

```
doskey
```

Just some of the useful facilities offered by DOSKEY include:

1. Access to all DOS commands already issued in the current session at the command prompt, by using the Up and Down arrow keys. When you see the one you want, simply press the Enter key. If you want to modify the command slightly before re-issuing it, use the Left and Right arrow keys to move through the command to edit it.

2. F7 key displays a list of all DOS commands used in the current session.

3. F9 key allows you to issue a command by selecting the relevant command number. These numbers are indicated in the list displayed when you press F7.

CONFIG.SYS

This is the second important file DOS uses. It stands for CONFIGuration of your SYStem. It allows you to specify new devices like a modem or a scanner you have attached to your PC, so that DOS knows about them. It also informs DOS about the maximum number of files or memory buffers your software will require.

Like the AUTOEXEC.BAT file, it may be updated automatically by any new software you install. You can again use the Editor to edit it yourself, and you have to re-boot or restart your computer to make the changes effective. A CONFIG.SYS file may look something like this:

```
device=c:\dos\setver.exe
device=c:\dos\himem.sys
dos=high
device=c:\dos\smartdrive.sys 2048
country=044,,c:\dos\country.sys
files=30
buffers=16
```

Commands in CONFIG.SYS

You will notice several statements starting with DEVICE. These define additional peripherals, like a scanner or a mouse, which have to be installed separately and do not exist on the main system board of your computer. Different devices are defined by specifying the driver name for it in the DEVICE statement. A driver is just a program telling DOS about a specific device. It usually has a file type or extension of .SYS, or sometimes .EXE.

Having said this, the first driver in our example, SETVER.EXE, is not for a hardware device. It is used to fool your software applications into thinking that they are using the version of DOS they were designed for. This is important because when a new version of DOS is released, not all your applications, like a word processor, will be updated overnight to use the new version efficiently. This software driver ensures that when you upgrade DOS, your applications continue to work as if nothing has changed.

The next driver, HIMEM.SYS, is used to make more memory available than the standard 1MB. This extra memory, above 1MB is called extended memory (it is described in more detail in Chapter 14).

DOS=HIGH will load most of DOS into the first 64K chunk of extended memory. This saves some conventional memory, as explained in Chapter 14.

The next bit is the SMARTDRV.SYS driver. This is used to provide a disk cache. It allows more of your program to be stored in memory rather than on disk. This improves the system performance because it is much faster to access information from memory than from a disk. In our example, the amount reserved for disk cache is 2048K or 2MB.

The next line, starting with COUNTRY, sets your machine to the national standard. The code, 044, is in fact the country code for the UK.

The FILES statement specifies the maximum number of files that any particular application will need to have open. It should be somewhere between 20 and 40. Most software will automatically increase this number on installation, if necessary.

Lastly, a "buffer" is a bit like a disk cache. It is a memory area that is used to store information accessed very frequently from the disk. The BUFFERS statement indicates the maximum number of buffers required.

Bypassing CONFIG.SYS and AUTOEXEC.BAT files

You may not wish to use some or all of your AUTOEXEC.BAT and CONFIG.SYS files. If you want to bypass both in their entirety when you start up your computer, press and release the F5 key or press and hold down the Shift key when the following text is displayed on the screen:

```
Starting MS-DOS...
```

This will display the message:

```
MS-DOS is bypassing your CONFIG.SYS and
AUTOEXEC.BAT files.
```

Your PC will start with the basic configuration instead of your usual one. If you do this, some of your system may not work as the approriate settings won't be used by the computer.

If you want to temporarily stop using a command in one of these files, prefix the command with REM, which stands for Remark. Any statement in the AUTOEXEC.BAT and CONFIG.SYS files which is prefixed with REM is ignored by the computer when it executes the files' instructions. You can use remark statements to add comments to explain what other statements in the files mean. This can be very useful if you have a complicated file with many instructions.

When you use CONFIG.SYS you can choose to confirm each command in the file before it is executed. This can be useful if you have a problem which you think may be related to your configuration. To do this, press and release F8 when the computer is displaying the following line after you have booted or turned on:

```
Starting MS-DOS...
```

DOS will display the message:

```
MS-DOS will prompt you to confirm each
CONFIG.SYS command.
```

Each line of the CONFIG.SYS file will then be displayed and you will be asked to type 'Y' or 'N' to have the line executed or not. When you have gone through all the commands, DOS will display the message:

```
Process AUTOEXEC.BAT [Y,N]?
```

Type 'Y' if you want the AUTOEXEC.BAT to be executed, or 'N' if you want it to be bypassed.

CHAPTER 14

Understanding your Computer's Memory

In this chapter you will learn ....

> About the different types of memory

> How to free memory and use memory managers

> What is SMARTDrive and how to use it

D OS manages and uses different types of memory in different ways. It is important to know how it does this to make effective use of your computer.

A little history

IBM designed and released the first PC in 1981. At that time, they did not think that anyone would ever need more than 640K of memory, or RAM to be more precise.

So they only reserved 1MB (1024K) memory, from which a maximum of 640K (called *conventional memory*) can be addressed and used by programs. The other 384K was reserved as video adapter memory, used to display screens. Since then there has never been a great demand for this memory and it remains wasted. This section of RAM is known as the *Upper Memory Area.*

As applications demanded more and more memory, a way had to be found to add memory and for DOS to be able to address and use it.

The MEM command

One solution was to use *extended memory*. This is extra memory above 1MB. If you are not sure whether you have any extended memory type:

```
C> mem
```

A typical output (taken from DOS 5.0) from the MEM command, assuming we have a CONFIG.SYS as shown in our example in Chapter 13, would be:

```
 655360    bytes total conventional memory
 655360    bytes available to MS-DOS
 592896    largest executable program size

3145728    bytes total contiguous extended memory
      0    bytes available contiguous extended memory
 983040    bytes available XMS
           MS-DOS resident in High Memory Area
```

The 655360 bytes of conventional memory is the standard 640K (655360 divided by 1024). From this 579K (592896 divided by 1024) is the maximum size available for any program. This means that you cannot run a program larger than this size. The remaining 61K is reserved for FILES and BUFFER statements (see Chapter 13), and for DOS itself.

The next line tells you that there is 3145728 bytes or 3MB of extended memory available. The zero just means that none of it is being managed at this time. Only 983040 bytes (960K) of extended memory is still available. This is because out of the

3MB total, 2MB is reserved for disk caching as specified by the SMARTDrive.SYS driver in our CONFIG.SYS file.

The remaining 64K of extended memory is taken up with DOS, with the DOS=HIGH statement in the CONFIG.SYS. This is the first block of extended memory, referred to as High Memory Area (HMA). Few programs use this area, so it is a good idea to load DOS into it to save space in conventional memory.

Extended versus Expanded

Extended memory is contiguous memory that can be accessed all at once, as required. It can be installed on any PC with a 286 processor or higher.

The other type of memory that can be added to your standard 1MB memory is called *expanded memory*. Unlike extended memory, it can be added to any PC, regardless of the processor used.

Expanded memory is also different in that it can only be accessed and exploited in blocks of 64K (called a *page*).

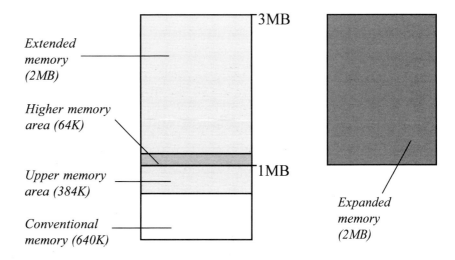

Extended memory (2MB)

Higher memory area (64K)

Upper memory area (384K)

Conventional memory (640K)

3MB

1MB

Expanded memory (2MB)

Blocks of 64K memory are "paged" in and out of standard memory from a "pool" of expanded memory, as necessary. This paging process makes accessing expanded memory a slower process than accessing extended memory.

The major drawback of expanded memory is that it cannot be used by all software. Windows does not use expanded memory, but can simulate it for running DOS-based applications which need it.

MemMaker

This command is used to manage your Upper Memory Area, which is not used for very much other than for display adapters. Therefore MemMaker loads some of your device drivers and other memory-resident programs into the Upper Memory Area. This frees up conventional memory for your programs to run in.

If you use the EMM386 memory manager in conjunction with Windows, you may not need to use MemMaker. EMM386 maps extended memory onto the Upper Memory Area as Windows wants as much extended memory as possible.

To use MemMaker type:

```
C> memmaker
```

This will display the Welcome screen for MemMaker. Press Enter and then choose Express or Custom Setup. In most cases MemMaker will free up space simply by using the Express setup, so choose this by pressing Enter again.

At the next screen, press Enter (to choose No) if you don't have any programs which require expanded memory or if you don't know whether you do. If you know you have programs which use expanded memory, press the spacebar to select Yes and then press Enter.

MemMaker will now tell you it's ready to restart your computer. Press Enter to let it do so. As each of your drivers and memory-resident programs starts, MemMaker watches and determines the optimum configuration for your computer. When it has done so it makes the necessary alterations to your AUTOEXEC.BAT and CONFIG.SYS files.

Freeing Conventional memory

Conventional memory is used by device drivers and by your application software such as a wordprocessor. Some of these need a lot of memory. Infact the memory requirement stated on software packages refers to this conventional memory. When you are running short of conventional memory you will need to free some space. There are several ways you can achieve this:

First of all, you can check your AUTOEXEC.BAT and CONFIG.SYS to ensure that you are not running any unnecessary memory-resident programs on startup.

Secondly, you can use the MemMaker command to load some of your device drivers into the Upper Memory Area.

If your computer has extended memory you can have DOS run in the high memory area. If you want to see whether your computer has DOS running in the High Memory Area, use the MEM command. This will display the line "MS-DOS is resident in the high memory area" if this is the case.

If you don't have DOS running in the high memory area, add the following lines to your CONFIG.SYS file:

```
device=c:\dos\himem.sys
dos=high
```

These commands load the HIMEM.SYS memory manager and then loads DOS into the High Memory Area.

Freeing Extended memory

Some programs, particularly Windows and Windows-based programs need to use extended memory. There are several ways to free up your computers' extended memory for these programs.

If you have programs which run in the upper memory area to conserve conventional memory, try running them in conventional memory instead. This will allow your extended memory manager, EMM386, to use free upper memory blocks as though they were extended memory. The simplest way to do this is to add REM to the start of the line in your CONFIG.SYS which has the EMM386 command in it. This will disable EMM386 and free up the unused upper memory blocks.

Look at your CONFIG.SYS and AUTOEXEC.BAT files to see whether you start any programs which use extended memory. You can reduce the amount of memory allocated to these programs to free it for other programs.

Also ensure that if the EMM386.EXE line in CONFIG.SYS does not contain the switch 'noems', then add the 'min=0' switch to the line. If you don't have the noems switch EMM386 reserves some of your extended memory to simulate expanded memory. If you choose the min=0 switch, EMM386 can still use extended memory to simulate expanded memory, but only does it when an application specifically needs it.

Use SMARTDrive (described soon) rather than RAMDrive to create a disk cache. On most drives, SMARTDrive speeds drive access more than RAMDrive anyway!

Freeing Expanded memory

Some programs need expanded memory and you can free it up to run them with, using a variety of methods.

First of all, you should ensure that your CONFIG.SYS file contains a 'device' command for the expanded memory manager which comes with your expanded memory board.

If you have any programs in your AUTOEXEC.BAT or CONFIG.SYS files that are allocated expanded memory, reduce the amount they are allocated or disable them using the REM command at the start of the line.

If you have extended memory, you can use EMM386 to use it to simulate expanded memory. Also, you should ensure that the EMM386 command line in CONFIG.SYS has the 'ram' switch after it and not the 'noems' switch, which means that expanded memory is not available.

SMARTDrive

SMARTDrive is a program which decreases the time it takes to read data from your hard disk. It reserves a section of extended memory to act as a cache. Applications can read from this cache much faster than from the hard disk. When your computer resources are occupied, SMARTDrive can also store information which is to be saved in the hard disk cache and write it to the disk when resources become available.

To use SMARTDrive each time you turn on your computer, add the following command to the end of your AUTOEXEC.BAT file:

```
smartdrv xxx [xxx]
```

For 'xxx', you should type the amount of your memory to be reserved for this cache. The amount for '[xxx]' is the value the cache should be reduced to if you use Windows, which itself needs to use as much extended memory as possible. The table on the next page shows the optimum values for these amounts, depending on how much extended memory you have.

Amount of extended memory	Cache size	Windows cache size
Up to 1MB	All extended memory	Zero
Up to 2MB	1MB	256K
Up to 4MB	1MB	512K
Up to 6MB	2MB	1MB
Over 6MB	2MB	2MB

Using DOS memory managers

These are device drivers which allow access to and control of particular types of memory, such as expanded or extended. You do not need to worry about managing conventional memory as DOS does that for you.

The two memory managers which are included with DOS are HIMEM and EMM386. HIMEM allows you to use extended memory and is installed automatically when you install DOS, if you have a 286 processor or higher.

EMM386 provides access to the upper memory area and lets you use extended memory to simulate expanded memory. To see whether you have EMM386.EXE running look at your CONFIG.SYS file and see whether there is a line including EMM386.EXE. If this is not the case, then the easiest way to install EMM386 is to run MemMaker, as described earlier, which will install and configure it for you.

HANDY TIP

Any expanded memory you have on your computer also needs to be managed and this is done by the memory manager which comes with the memory board. There needs to be a command in your CONFIG.SYS file to load the memory manager. The documentation relating to your expanded memory board will explain this command in more detail, as each memory manager is specially designed for the particular memory board.

Securing against
Loss of Data

In this chapter you will learn ....

➤ About backing up your files on floppy disks

➤ How to restore backed-up files

➤ About methods of protecting data against viruses

➤ About ways of recovering files you have deleted

P rotecting the information you have on your PC cannot be over-emphasised. Sooner or later you will encounter a problem and may lose work which has taken hours, days or even months to compile.

The most common cause of data loss is human error. You can easily type the wrong command and wipe off things you did not mean to. Next comes data loss because of hardware or software failure. If your computer suddenly packs up when you are in the middle of an application, some files may get corrupted. A bug in a new release of a software package you bought, or a virus you may have inherited by copying files from outsiders, may also do strange things to your data. The last and often overlooked case is when the data storage medium itself is damaged or lost by theft or natural disasters such as fire or flood.

If these problems occur you will want to be able to recover from them. This chapter shows you how to do this.

Backing up your files

Hard disk drives have a life-span which averages around five years, although it will vary from make to make. Eventually any hard disk drive will fail and when it does, anything stored on it is likely to be lost. Obviously, this is a very serious problem.

To safeguard yourself against this problem, you should take regular backups from your hard disk. A backup is a copy of files from your hard disk to floppy disks. If you keep regular backups and then have a hard disk problem you will be able to restore the files saved in your last back up. This way, you will only lose the work you have done since that backup.

One thing to remember is that floppy disks can fail or be damaged too. To be safe, you should have several backup sets. If you have three sets, for example, you could cycle through them, so that if one set of floppies gets damaged or fails, you will have two other (older) sets to work from (this 3-set backup procedure is known as a Grandfather, Father and Son cycle).

Before you start backing up, you need to decide which files you will back up and how often you will do it.

The more files you backup the more time and floppy disks it takes. You may decide that you don't need to back up all your files, just the most important ones or those that would take most time to replace.

The more often you backup, the more up to date the saved versions of your files will be. If you create/update lots of files each day, a daily backup may be called for. If you don't, you may only need to backup once a week, or even once a month.

Different types of backups

There are three types of backups you can do:

A *full backup* is one in which you backup the complete contents of all the selected files. This can be time consuming if you need to back up a lot of files.

An *incremental backup* is where you backup only the files that have changed since your last full or incremental backup. You need to keep each incremental backup copy as they build on each other. This backup strategy is best if you work with lots of files and want to preserve multiple versions of them. You make a full backup and then make subsequent incremental backups to keep a continuous record of your files. Eventually you should perform another full backup and start the cycle again.

Finally, there are *differential backups* where you back up only the files which have changed since your last full backup. This preserves only the latest version of the files. Differential backups are best if you work with the same files regularly but only want to preserve the current version. In this type of backup you only need to keep your original full Backup and the latest differential backup.

How to backup your files

If you are using DOS version 6.0 or higher there is an easier way to perform backups. When you install DOS you are given the choice of installing the DOS version of Backup, the Windows version, or both. Select the Backup icon from the Microsoft Tools group to use the Windows version, or type

the following command at the command prompt to use the
DOS version:

```
C> msbackup
```

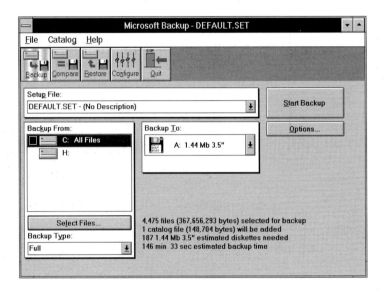

The backup screen will be displayed. The DOS and Windows
screens are very similar and the Windows version is shown
above.

You can choose to backup the whole of your hard drive
(which will take a lot of time and floppy disks, but which may
be necessary if you have lots of valuable files) by double
clicking on the drive icon (usually C) in the Backup From box.

You can select certain files or directories to be backed up. To
do this click on the drive you wish to back up files from. Then
click on the Select Files... button and a screen will be
displayed showing a directory tree and a list of files. Clicking
on a directory will list the files in that directory. If you click
on a directory with a '+' sign folder, it will expand to show its
subdirectories.

Double click on a directory name to select all the files in that directory for backup, or just highlight the directory (click on it once) and press the spacebar. If you only want to backup some files, then either double click on the files you want or press the spacebar key to select highlighted files.

If you change your mind about the directories and files you have selected for backup, simply double-click with your mouse or press the spacebar key again to de-select specific directories/files.

Click on the Backup Type box and select whether you want a Full, Incremental or Differential backup. Click on the Backup To box and select the drive where you want to backup to, which will normally be your 'A' floppy disk drive.

You can keep a backup on your hard disk, but this obviously won't save you if it fails itself.

If you are likely to back up the same files repeatedly, as in the case of incremental backups, you can save your list of selected files and backup parameters by selecting the Save Setup As choice from the File menu. When you come to do your next backup, click on the Setup File box and select the file with your saved backup choices.

To begin your backup, click on the Start Backup button and your computer will display how far the backup has progressed and when to insert your floppy disks for backup.

Backup compatibility test

The first time you use backup, a message will be displayed telling you that you need to perform a compatibility test. The message will be displayed each time you start backup until you perform the test.

To start the compatibility test, press Enter (or click on OK if you are using the Windows version) and follow the instructions on the screen. The software will run a small backup and then compare the backed up files to the originals, to ensure that backup is set up correctly to use your computer's hardware.

If you change the hardware of your computer (by adding a new mouse or disk drive, for example), you should choose Configure from the main backup screen and update your systems configuration.

Comparing backed up files

Once you have made a backup copy of your files; you can ensure that it is identical to your original files by using Compare. It is useful to compare your backed up files to their orignals to ensure that there are no minor hardware problems in the disk drives that might slightly alter your backed up files.

To compare files, click on the Compare button on the main Backup screen. This will display the Compare screen from which you can choose which files to compare and then click on the Start Compare button.

You can also use Compare at any time to see how many differences there are between your backup copy of files and the versions on the hard disk to determine whether you need to backup again. The more changes you find the more necessary a new backup becomes.

Restoring backed up files

Once you have made a backup you may, at a future date, need to restore the backed up files to your hard disk. This is done using the Restore option in Backup. You can choose to restore the whole set of files on your floppy disks or just some of them.

To access Restore, click on the Restore button on the main Backup screen. The Restore screen will be displayed and you can choose which version of your backed up files to use by clicking on Restore From. You can also click on Select Files to choose particular files if you don't want to restore all of them.

If you click on Restore To you can choose where to put the restored files. Clicking on the Start Restore button will start prompting you to insert your backup disks one by one and also display the progress as files are being restored.

Scanning for viruses

Computer viruses are programs which are designed to replicate themselves and spread through computer systems. They are a growing problem as more and more are written and they become increasingly sophisticated. Some viruses are relatively harmless, but others can be very dangerous to your computer's health. DOS includes a command called Anti-Virus which can detect viruses and deal with them.

Anti-Virus is another DOS command which can also be used from Windows. If it is installed in Windows, double-click on the Anti-Virus icon in the Microsoft Tools group.

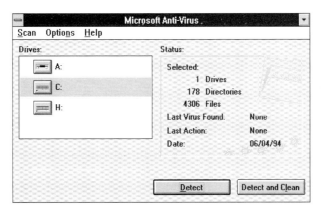

If you are using Anti-Virus from DOS, type:

```
C> msav
```

Both the DOS and Windows versions use similar Anti-Virus screens. First, you should select the drive you wish to check for viruses in by clicking on it.

Choose Detect if you just want Anti-Virus to look for viruses. If it finds one, it will ask you whether you want the virus removed or ignored, the file where the virus has been found deleted, or the virus scan stopped.

Choose Detect and Clean if you want Anti-Virus to search for viruses and remove them automatically.

If you want Anti-Virus to scan your computer's memory and drives each time you turn on your machine, add the following line in the AUTOEXEC.BAT file.

```
C> msav /p
```

If you want to find out about one of the viruses that Anti-Virus can detect, press F9 and the virus list will be displayed. Select the virus you want to find out about and click on Info. Information about the selected virus will then be displayed.

VSafe

Often prevention is better than cure. This is how VSafe can help. It is a memory-resident program, constantly monitoring for activity which might indicate the presence of a virus. When VSafe finds such an activity it displays a warning. To run VSafe, type the following at the command prompt:

```
C> vsafe
```

If you want VSafe to begin running each time you start your computer type VSAFE in your AUTOEXEC.BAT file.

Delete protection

Delete protection can help you to avoid losing information if you accidentally delete a file. Undelete has three levels of delete protection and the success of attempts to undelete files (described in Chapter 4) can depend on the level of protection they are given.

The three levels of delete protection are Delete Sentry, Delete Tracker and Standard.

Delete Sentry gives the best protection, but it takes up a small amount of disk space and memory. It stores the deleted files in a hidden directory rather than deleting them as normal. Files which are protected using Delete Sentry can usually be recovered without difficulty.

Delete Tracker provides a lower level of protection. It takes up less disk space than Delete Sentry, but requires the same amount of memory. Files protected using Delete Tracker may be partly overwritten and so corrupted.

Standard protection does not require any disk space or memory and provides the least protection.

The level of delete protection can be assigned at the command prompt or through the Windows version of Undelete (select from the Microsoft Tools group window). By default, DOS uses the Standard protection, so if you wish your files to be better protected, you have to tell DOS to use your preferred level of delete protection. To do this in the Windows version, select Configure Delete Protection from the Options menu and choose the required level of protection.

To use Delete Sentry protection directly through DOS, type the following at the command prompt:

```
C> undelete /s
```

and for Delete Tracker, type:

```
C> undelete /tc
```

where the '/t' switch represents Tracker and the 'c' represents the drive to be protected.

To have these Delete protection systems run automatically each time you turn on your computer, add one of the commands just described to your AUTOEXEC.BAT file.

Undeleting your files

You may find you have accidentally deleted an important file. Don't panic! Undelete may be able to recover it for you. The DOS version of Undelete was described in Chapter 4, but here the Windows version, which is available with version 6.0 onwards, is explained.

When you delete a file it is not destroyed, but the space it occupies can then be used for storing other files. The longer you delay after deleting a file before restoring it, the more likely it is that something will have over-written some or all of the deleted file. Therefore you should try and use Undelete immediately after you delete a file.

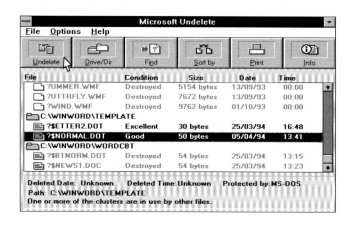

When you install DOS, you are given the choice of installing the DOS version of Undelete, the Windows version or both. To use Undelete in Windows, double-click on the Undelete icon in the Microsoft Tools group. The Undelete screen will then appear.

Click on Drive/Dir to display a screen where you can select the drive or directory to be searched for deleted files. Click on OK and Undelete looks for files that have been deleleted and displays them. The list includes an indicator of the state of the file. The conditions range from perfect to destroyed and this will tell you whether your file can be recovered.

Condition	Which means...
Perfect	The file was protected by Delete Sentry and can be recovered without difficulty.
Excellent	The file was protected by Delete Tracker and may have been partly overwritten.
Good	The file is fragmented on the disk and some of the data may have been overwritten.
Poor	The file has been overwritten and cannot be recovered using Undelete for Windows. Undelete for MS-DOS may recover some of it.
Destroyed	The file cannot be recovered.

In the case of files in poor condition, Undelete for DOS may be able to recover the file, but Undelete for Windows won't be able to. In all other cases the DOS and Windows versions function similarly.

To recover a file, click on it to select it and then click on Undelete. You will be asked to type the initial letter of the filename and Undelete will then recover your file.

If you wish to use Undelete from the command prompt, refer to Chapter 4.

If you have version 5.0 of DOS, you will have to use the MIRROR command to keep track of files deleted. To monitor files deleted in drives A, B and C type:

```
C> mirror c:/ta/tb/tc
```

Add this line to the AUTOEXEC.BAT file if you want to have MIRROR monitor deleted files every time you use your computer.

Even if Undelete manages to recover a file, you should always check to see whether it has been damaged, as it may not have been recovered intact. If a recovered file is damaged, you can correct the damage but if it is too badly damaged you will have to create the file from scratch again.

If Undelete proves incapable of recovering a file, you could restore a backup copy (if you have one) stored on floppy disks. Recovering deleted files in this way is another good reason for having backups.

A Special Reference for Novices

This is the section you'll want to keep referring to once you have read the book. It highlights and explains the error messages DOS is likely to throw at you. You'll then find a chapter of DOS commands grouped in order of importance. Details like the version in which a command first appeared and a cross-reference for it in the book are given so that you can easily decide if a particular command is valid for your version of DOS and which page to read for more details on how to use the command. Useful tips about using your computer and summary of popular DOS commands and keys are also provided.

Common DOS Error Messages (and what to do about them)

In this chapter you will learn ....

> What the error messages mean

> What you can do to sort out the problems

> Some of the mistakes you might make

■ ■

Microsoft stopped providing a reference for all DOS error messages in their manuals from version 4.0. Since most of the messages are vague it is very difficult, especially for a beginner, to know what they mean and how to get round them.

This chapter addresses this problem and explains the error messages you are likely to encounter.

Abort, Retry, Ignore?

This message applies to a few situations. It is usually displayed because you are trying to read from, or write to, a floppy disk and there isn't one inserted or the disk drive is not closed properly. Type R for Retry after inserting a disk properly or A for Abort to cancel the command.

Access denied

Displayed if you are trying to change, rename or delete a
"read-only" protected file. Either don't alter the file because
it's probably an important system file that should not be
altered, or change the file attribute so that it's no longer read-
only. See *Changing File Attributes*, Chapter 9.

Bad command or file name

DOS does not recognise the command you have just typed.
Usually it's caused because you made a typing or spelling
mistake. Simply re-type the command and try again.

Drive not ready

Also "Not ready, reading drive x". As expected, these
messages appear when you've tried to access a floppy disk
drive when a disk is not yet properly inserted.

Duplicate file name

Occurs when you try to rename a file to a name that already
exists or the file you are trying to rename does not exist.
Check for both file names and try again.

File cannot be copied onto itself

Displayed when you use a copy command and specify the same
name for the source and destination. Often you mean to keep
the same name but want to copy the file to another disk or
directory and have simply forgotten to type this path in the
destination part of the command.

File not found

DOS cannot find the file you have specified in a command. Check the path and spelling of the file name. If you still don't have any luck refer to *Finding a lost File* in Chapter 9.

Format failure

Displayed if you tried to format a defective disk. Use another disk.

Insufficient disk space

You don't have enough space on the disk to save or copy a new or updated file. Either delete some old files first to create the space or use another disk.

Insufficient memory

There isn't enough memory to load the program you typed to run. You may need to upgrade the memory in your computer to conform to the minimum that the program requires to run (see the documentation that came with the program) or there may be some memory-resident (also called TSR) programs that need to be un-installed first to make room for the new program.

Invalid directory

A directory you have specified in a DOS command does not exist. Check the spelling or use the TREE command to display the names of all directories.

Invalid drive specification

A disk drive letter that DOS does not know about was used. Normally the letter A is used for your floppy disk drive, B for your second floppy disk drive if you have one, and C for the hard disk. Other letters are used if you have a CD-ROM drive or if your computer is connected to others on a network and you have access to disks on other machines (network drives).

Check that the correct drive letter is used, followed by a colon (:).

Invalid file name

You've named a file using one of the illegal characters listed in Chapter 9 under *Naming conventions*. Retype the name correctly using a maximum of 8 valid characters for the name and 3 for the extension.

Invalid number of parameters
Invalid parameter
Invalid path

These are some more 'Invalid...' messages. They usually all occur because you have forgotten to type a bit of the command or made a typing error. Check the format of the command (using HELP *command* at the DOS prompt).

Non-system disk or disk error

You've tried to start your computer with a non-system floppy disk inserted in drive A. Although most computers now have hard disks and the operating system (DOS) is installed on the hard disk, early machines only had floppy drives and DOS had to be loaded into memory from a floppy disk. Due to upward-compatibility even today your system will look to load DOS from the A floppy disk drive first. If there is no disk inserted it will automatically then go on to search your hard disk. However if it finds a floppy disk then this message is displayed. Simply remove the floppy disk and start your computer again.

Write protect

You are trying to save a new file or change/delete a file from a disk that is write-protected. See *Write-protecting a floppy* in Chapter 6.

A Quick Tour
of DOS Commands

In this chapter you will learn ....

> What each command does

> In which version of DOS it first appeared

> Where the command is decribed in this book

> Whether the commands are external or internal

D OS is upward-compatible. This means that the version numbers given here, for each command, allow you to use that command in that version of DOS as well as all future versions. If you have an older version of DOS than that stated here, you will need to upgrade your DOS to use that particular command on your system.

The commands are divided up into sections which show how often you are likely to use them and show which commands are not available in recent versions of DOS.

The Type column lists an 'I' if the command is internal and an 'E' if it is external. See Chapter 3 for an explanation of internal and external commands.

Everyday commands

These are the commands you are likely to use most often. They are on the whole for basic file and directory handling.

Command	Type	Version	See Page	Description
CD	I	2.0	28, 90	CHDIR achieves the same. Used to change to a different directory.
COPY	I	1.0	38-40	Copies files across to any directory, drive or device. You can also use it to rename the file at the same time.
DEL	I	1.0	42	Deletes unwanted files. Same as the ERASE command.
DIR	I	1.0	24-25	Displays the directory of files on the disk.
FORMAT	E	1.0	68-73, 78	Prepares disks for use.
HELP	E	5.0	30	Displays help on any DOS command. You can just type the command followed by a /? switch to get help on a specific command. e.g. DIR /?
MD	I	2.0	90	MKDIR achieves the same. Used to make or create a new directory.
MORE	E	2.0	106, 121	Controls the display on your screen so that when there is a screenful of information, an automatic pause is initiated.
MOVE	I	6.0	40-41	Moves files from one location to another. Can be used to rename files.

RD	I	**2.0**	**91**	RMDIR achieves the same. Used to remove or delete a directory. This will only work if there are no files in the directory you want to remove.
REN	I	**1.0**	**41-42**	RENAME (in full) can be used too. They both rename a file to a new name.
TYPE	I	**1.0**	**26, 44**	Displays a file on the screen.

Useful commands

These are commands you will find yourself using a lot. They include some slightly more complicated file commands, general disk commands and several basic DOS facilities.

Command	Type	Version	See Page	Description
CLS	I	**2.0**	**30**	Used from the command prompt, it CLears the Screen and redisplays the prompt at the top left corner of the screen.
DATE	I	**1.0**	**28-29**	Displays and sets the system date.
DELTREE	I	**6.0**	**89**	Deletes an entire directory including the files and subdirectories it contains.
DOSKEY	E	**5.0**	**33, 126**	A utility which allows you to redisplay and re-issue previously used DOS commands from the command prompt.
DOSSHELL	E	**4.0**	**48**	Loads the easy to use, menu-driven shell. You will be able to perform many common DOS functions through this interface.

EDIT	E	5.0	**45, 124**	This is the new full-screen text editor. It is used to edit just text (also called ASCII) files. It replaces the old EDLIN.
ERASE	I	1.0	**42**	Same as DEL.
EXIT	E	2.0	**51, 116**	If you were only temporarily working at the command prompt from either the DOS shell or Windows, it will return you to the appropriate environment. It also returns you to the original copy of DOS if you had started to run another copy using COMMAND.
FIND	E	2.0	**121-122**	Locates a word or several words in a file or group of files.
LABEL	E	3.1	**71**	Creates, changes or deletes the volume label on a disk.
MSBACKUP	E	6.0	**144**	Copies files from hard disk onto floppies, should you have any hard disk problems.
PATH	I	2.0	**87-88**	Used to specify the directories to be searched to find a program that you will want to run frequently. It avoids the need to type the long-winded path name each time you want to access a program that is not in the current directory.
PRINT	E	2.0	**44-45**	Allows you to print text files. It also acts as a spooler, which means that it will queue print jobs if there are several to print, leaving you free to do other work on the PC.

SORT	E	2.0	121	Sorts lines within a file alphabetically.
TIME	I	1.0	29	Displays and allows you to change the system time.
TREE	E	3.2	88	Displays a hierarchy of directories on a disk.
VOL	I	2.0	71	Displays the volume label of a disk.
XCOPY	E	3.2	98-99	This is an eXtended COPY command. It provides more flexibility in selectively copying files and directories.

Once-in-a-while commands

These are also useful commands, but ones which you are only likely to use occasionally. They include more complicated file handling, data security, memory and disk commands.

Command	Type	Version	See Page	Description
ATTRIB	E	3.0	95-96	Changes the characteristics or attributes of files. eg "Read only" or "Archive".
CHKDSK	E	1.0	78-80	Short for CHecK DiSK. It is used to check your disk space, including how much free space you still have. It also allows you to fix some errors on the disk and diplays the amount of conventional memory available.
DBLSPACE	E	6.0	81-82	Initiates a file compression routine which can increase your hard disk space by a factor of two.

DEFRAG	E	6.0	80	Locates separated fragments of files stored on disk and brings them together, thus speeding disk access.
DISKCOMP	E	3.2	74-75	Compares two floppy disks for an exact match. Use it to check that the DISKCOPY command worked.
DISKCOPY	E	2.0	73-74	Duplicates a whole disk onto another one. Usually used if you want an exact copy of a floppy disk on another. Both disks must be the same size and have the same capacity.
MEM	E	4.0	132-133	Displays all types of memory available on your system: conventional, expanded and extended.
MEMMAKER	E	6.0	134-135	Optimises conventional memory space by loading some memory-resident programs into the upper memory area.
MSAV	E	6.0	148	Scans the disk for viruses and can remove any that are found.
PROMPT	I	2.0	32-33	Changes the DOS command prompt so that it can be more useful to you.
SCANDISK	E	6.2	83	Checks the disk for errors and corrects them.
SMARTDRV	E	6.0	127-128, 137	Creates a disk cache in extended memory, which speeds up access to files.

SYS	E	**1.0**	**72**	Makes a disk a DOS systems disk by transfering system files to it.
UNDELETE	E	**5.0**	**43, 150-152**	Recovers a file that has been deleted by mistake.
VER	I	**2.0**	**29-30**	Displays the version number of your DOS.
VSAFE	E	**6.0**	**148**	Checks your hard disk and memory for evidence of virus activity while you work.

Rarely used commands

It is unlikely that you'll be using the commands described here.

Command	Type	Version	Description
APPEND	E	**3.2**	Used to specify directories that a program may need to search for files. Avoids the need to change the current directory.
BREAK	I	**2.0**	Allows you to press Ctrl+Break or Ctrl+C to cancel or interrupt the execution of a long program.
CHCP	I	**3.3**	Stands for CHange Code Page. This is effectively the character set. For example, CHCP 860 will change the character set your computer uses to Portuguese.
EXPAND	E	**5.0**	Uncompresses or expands a DOS file.
FC	E	**2.0**	File Compare. It is similar to the COMP command, but the output is more useful.
LH	E	**6.0**	Load High. Loads DOS or other memory-resident programs into the high memory area.

MODE	E	3.2	Used to configure peripherals (known as devices to DOS), like the printer, modem, screen, keyboard. It can be used to redirect output from one device to another or just to display the status of a particular device.
MSCDEX	E	6.0	Enables DOS to access CD-ROM drives.
REPLACE	E	3.2	Updates (replaces) files from one drive/directory to another if there is a match. Ensures that you are using an up-to-date set of files if more than one set exists.
SHARE	E	3.0	Reserves some disk space to store control information about files which are going to be shared in a network.
SUBST	E	3.1	SUBSTitutes a long directory name or path with a letter. It will save you typing a long path name everytime. Avoid using one of your disk drive letter.
UNFORMAT	E	5.0	Recovers lost information from a disk formatted by mistake.
VERIFY	E	6.0	Instructs DOS to verify whether your files have been written correctly to disk.

Difficult or dangerous commands

These commands are either complicated to use and therefore only suitable for experts, or may corrupt your files and disks if not used correctly. If you need to use these commands, it is recommended you get expert help.

Command	Type	Version	Description
COMMAND	E	1.0	Lets you run another copy of DOS on your machine. This executes the COMMAND.COM

program which is used to interpret commands you type at the keyboard.

CTTY	I	2.0	Stands for Change TeleTYpe. Your standard input device is the keyboard. You can change this to another device.
FASTOPEN	E	3.3	Stores the location of a number of most recently accessed files in memory, so that those files can be accessed much more quickly.
FDISK	E	3.2	Allows you to partition your fixed disk (also called a hard disk). Therefore, although you may only have one physical disk, logically you can divide it in two. Then use another drive letter (D for example) to access the second drive.

Discontinued and superceded commands

This last section lists those DOS commands which have become obsolete and therefore are replaced by newer ones in the latest version of DOS. They will exist in your version if your version of DOS is lower than the number given under the Removed column here.

Command	Type	Version	Removed	Description
ASSIGN	E	3.0	6.0	Allocates another disk drive letter to an existing disk drive.
BACKUP	E	2.0	6.0	Copies files usually from the hard disk to floppy disks. MSBACKUP now performs the same function.
COMP	E	3.3	6.0	COMPares two files character by character. Now replaced by the FC command.
EDLIN	E	1.0	5.0	A very basic LINe EDitor. It served the same purpose as EDIT, which is much better.

JOIN	E	3.1	6.0	Logically combines the contents of two disks fully or partially through using directories, so that they are treated as one by DOS.
MIRROR	E	5.0	6.0	Records information which may be required by the UNDELETE and UNFORMAT commands.
RECOVER	E	2.0	6.0	Tries to recover files that for some reason DOS cannot read.
RESTORE	E	2.0	-	Copies files back from a previous backup carried out using BACKUP. MSBACKUP (from 6.0) performs the same function. The RESTORE command is still available to use with files backed up prior to version 6.0.

Tips and Troubleshooting

In this chapter you will learn ....

➢ How to start up and shut down your computer correctly

➢ What to do if your computer won't start

➢ How to use your computer safely and efficiently

➢ DOS commands and important keys to remember

T here are certain basic things you should remember when working with DOS and your computer. This chapter outlines these and you should read them very carefully especially if you are relatively new to using computers.

While starting your computer

- Check there isn't a floppy disk inserted in your disk drive A.

- If you are going to be using peripherals like the printer, switch them on first, before starting your computer. If your monitor does not power up automatically from the computer, then turn it on before you turn on the main system unit.

- If your computer does not start properly, first switch it off and then check that all the cables are firmly connected. Then try again.

- If your keyboard doesn't work, check that you have not got your keyboard locked - most PCs have a keyboard-lock key at the front or side panel of the system unit. If the keyboard still doesn't respond, check that it is plugged in properly at the back and then start your computer again.

- If your monitor does not display anything, check that it does not have to be switched on separately from the system unit. If it is on, then check the brightness control.

- If you need to turn off your computer before switching it on again, wait at least ten seconds in between.

While working on your computer

- Don't take out a floppy disk from a disk drive when it's drive light is still on.

- Don't switch off your computer when the hard disk (C) drive light is still on.

- Don't re-boot or reset your computer while an application is running.

- Don't switch off your computer to end an application.

- Don't connect or re-connect any devices or peripherals into your computer until you have switched it off.

- Don't format your hard disk.

- Don't format a floppy disk to a different storage capacity than what it was designed for.

Care and handling of your floppy disks

- Don't leave your floppy disks in direct sunlight.

- Don't take your floppy disks near a magnet or devices that have a magnet inside them.

- Don't get your floppy disks wet.

- Don't write on the disk label after it's stuck - try and do it before you stick the label on the disk.

- Don't expose the magnetic disk surface to dust particles in the air and never touch it.

Care of your computer

- Don't leave your computer in direct sunlight.

- Don't keep the back of your computer right up against a wall.

- Don't keep your computer in a stuffy un-ventilated room.

- Don't spill coffee or smoke near your computer.

Proper procedure for shutting down

- Exit properly from the application you are using. e.g select Exit from the File menu within an application.

- Exit from the DOS shell or Windows if you were running your application from within one of these environments.

- At the DOS command prompt type PARK if your hard disk does not have an auto-park feature.

- Flick the On/Off switch to Off or press the On/Off button depending on the type of computer you have.

- If you need to switch your computer On again, wait a while - don't do it straight away.

Quick command reference

Change drives
From any drive to drive A...**A:**
From any drive to drive C... **C:**

Directory commands
Display the current directory.. **DIR**
Display another directory............................. **DIR \ANOTHER**
Display another drive's directory................................ **DIR A:**
Pause the directory list after each screen-page............. **DIR /P**
Display the directory in wide format.........................**DIR /W**
Display the current directory name.....................................**CD**
Change to another directory............................**CD ANOTHER**
Make a new directory...................................... **MD NEWDIR**
Remove an empty directory.............................**RD EMPDIR**
Remove a whole directory branch..........**DELTREE BRANCH**

File commands
Make a duplicate copy of a file...............**COPY FILE1 FILE2**
Copy a file to another drive...........................**COPY FILE1 A:**
Copy a file from another drive.......................**COPY A:FILE1**
Copy a file to another directory......**COPY FILE1 \ANOTHER**
Copy a group of files...................................**COPY *.DOC A:**
Delete a file...**DEL FILE1**
Delete all files in a directory....................................**DEL *.***
Rename a file... **REN FILE1 FILE2**
Display the contents of a file...............................**TYPE FILE1**

Disk commands

Format a disk in drive A....................................**FORMAT A:**
Format a low-density 5¼" disk............... **FORMAT A: /F:360**
Format a low-densisty 3½" disk...............**FORMAT A: /F:720**
Change a disk's volume label................................ **LABEL A:**

Useful keys to remember

BACKSPACE....................................erases characters typed
Ctrl+X.....................cancels the whole line of command typed
Ctrl+C...cancels a DOS command
Ctrl+S...............pauses the display (press any key to continue)
F3...................................repeats the last DOS command issued
ENTER ....sends the command typed to be interpreted

Glossary

Application programs
Programs designed to perform specific business functions like accounting and wordprocessing, rather than internal system functions of your computer.

ASCII
An acronym for *American Standard Code for Information Interchange*. It is the agreed standard representing all the characters and symbols inside your computer. Also refers to 'raw' text without any formatting; used to transfer data from one application to another.

AUTOEXEC.BAT
A special file used to 'batch' together several DOS commands that are executed every time the PC is started up. DOS looks for this file when the PC is started up and automatically follows the commands that are contained in it.

Backslash (\ )
In DOS, the backslash is used to indicate the *root* directory, as well as a separator between directories and file in a pathname. Don't confuse it with a *forward slash* (/).

Backup
A DOS command or a procedure to create a copy of programs or data. It is usual to hold this spare (backup) copy on a different storage medium (usually a floppy disk) from the original (usually the hard disk). The backup copy can then be used if the original is lost or damaged.

Bit
Short for BInary digiT. A bit is a binary digit '0' or '1'. Computers only work in binary digits. A character or a *byte* is represented by eight bits internally.

Boot
To boot a computer means to start a computer. The process involves switching it on and having it load up the operating system such as DOS. Re-boot means to re-start or reset.

Buffer
This is memory area used to store information which is accessed frequently from the disk. Buffers are used to speed-up disk accesses.

Byte
A byte consists of eight *bits* and it also represents storage for one character.

CD ROM

An acronym for compact disc read only memory. Just like the CD's used to store music, CD ROMs are portable optical storage devices. Information recorded on them cannot usually be changed, but they do offer massive storage capacity.

CMOS

Stands for *complimentary metal oxide semiconductor*. Battery powered memory, within the computer, used to maintain the clock and store information on the system configuration.

Command

An instruction telling DOS to do something. Also referred to as DOS command.

COMMAND.COM

A file listing commonly used DOS commands which is automatically loaded into memory when DOS is loaded. The commands in this file are called internal commands.

Compression

A mathematical technique by which information is stored in a denser form than usual (to save disk storage space).

CONFIG.SYS

A text file that DOS looks for when the system is started. It holds information on the system set-up and configuration, such as how to communicate with various pieces of hardware.

Conventional memory

The first 640 kilobytes of the basic one megabyte of memory on a PC.

Data

Raw figures or characters a program processes. e.g. accounts figures.

Default

When there is more than one choice available, many programs are designed to assume a designated value, should you fail to specify one. This is known as the default value. e.g. if you don't specify the disk drive, DOS will assume you mean the current drive (the drive that you are using now).

Device drivers

Programs that control the configuration and use of the various hardware devices, such as the monitor, mouse, printer and keyboard.

Dialog box

An area of the screen that is displayed when you are expected to provide some information.

Directory

A logical section of a disk. Usually a directory will contain files of a similar type or on a related subject.

Directory tree
The structure of directories and sub-directories on a disk.

Disk
A media used for permanent storage of computer based data and programs. Most disks have a magnetic coating on which the data is recorded.

Disk cache
An area of memory used to hold a copy of frequently used data. It is quicker for the processor to access data from memory rather than from the hard disk. *Disk caching* is a way of increasing processing time by saving on access time.

Disk drive
A disk drive is part of the *system unit* of a computer. It holds disks, reads data from disks and writes data on disks. A disk drive and a disk must be compatible in terms of physical size and capacity.

DOS
The *Disk Operating System* is a program that controls the activities of your computer.

DOS memory
Refers to *conventional memory*.

DOS Shell
A *graphical user interface* which can be used to perform common DOS functions.

DR-DOS
A version of DOS from Digital Research.

Edit
A DOS editor that allows you to change a text-based file.

Error message
A message output by DOS to tell you that something has gone wrong or that a command has not been executed properly.

Expanded memory
Memory that can be added to the basic one megabyte that DOS can address. Expanded memory can be added to any PC, but cannot be used by all software. It is accessed in 64K segments known as *pages*, making it slower to use than other types of memory.

Expansion card/slot
An expansion card is a circuit board that can be fitted inside your computer, as long as you have at least one expansion slot free on the motherboard. Required for adding hardware such as memory and CD-ROM to your system.

Extended memory
Continuous memory added to the basic one megabyte memory that DOS can address. Extended memory can be accessed and manipulated as required. It can be installed on a computer with a 286 or higher processor which most have

nowadays. Extended memory is used by Windows and it is the most common type of extra memory used today.

Extension
The last three letters of a file name which come after the "." (dot). It is used to indicate the type of information stored in the file or the software that created it.

External command
A DOS command which is not contained within the COMMAND.COM file and which must be loaded into memory before it can be executed.

File
A collection of information held together under one entity. The information may be a program, or something you create using an application such as a wordprocessor or spreadsheet.

Filter
A DOS command allowing information in a file to be sorted or modified.

Floppy disk
A permanent form of storage medium that may be separated from the computer. There are two basic types available for the PC: 5.25" and 3.5". The latter is made with a stronger casing and has a higher storage capacity.

Format
A DOS command or a process of preparing disks for use. Formatting a disk involves dividing it up and allocating areas for data storage.

Forward slash (/)
In DOS, the forward slash is used to specify a switch or an option to tailor a particular command.

Gigabyte
A billion *bytes* (1,073,741,824 precisely) or characters.

Hard disk
A permanent storage medium, usually fixed inside the computer. Hence it is also sometimes called a *fixed disk*. It has a far higher capacity and it is much more efficient to use than a *floppy disk*. For any serious work, you will need to have a hard disk on your system.

Hardware
The physical parts of your system such as the keyboard, VDU and the printer.

Higher memory area
The first 64 kilobytes of *extended memory* not used by most software; and into which DOS can be loaded to save space in *conventional memory*.

Installation
Usually involves copying a sofware package purchased onto your system, carrying out initial settings and modifications to the *system files* at the

same time. An automatic install or setup program is usually included with your software. You can also install hardware components in your computer like a *network card.*

Internal command
One of the DOS commands which is contained in the COMMAND.COM file and which is loaded into memory automatically when DOS is loaded.

K
Short for Kilobyte. It is 1024 bytes or characters of storage.

Keyboard
The main hardware device for entering data in a computer. A computer keyboard looks very much like a typewriter keyboard, but has extra keys for specific computer functions.

Load
Involves moving a program or data into the computer's memory, usually from disk.

Macro
A key or a command set up to represent a sequence of keystrokes or commands.

MB
Short for Megabyte. It is approximately a thousand *Kilobytes* or a million characters (1,048,576 to be precise).

Memory
What the computer uses to store information it is working on. There are different types of memory, which DOS accesses in different ways. They are *Conventional, Extended* and *Expanded.*

Memory cache
An expensive type of memory which can be read and written to at a much faster rate than the ordinary memory. Used to hold 'live' information that is used frequently by the processor. The overall benefit of *memory caching* is that programs work at much faster speeds.

Memory manager
A program which allows access to a particular type of memory and which allocates sections of the memory to different activities and programs.

Memory-resident programs
Programs that are designed to stay in memory next to DOS until called for. Many of the utility programs are memory resident. They sit in the memory until a pre-defined key combination is pressed to activate them. Also known as *TSR -* terminate and stay resident - programs.

Menu
A list of commands or options displayed on screen, prompting you to select one.

Mouse

An input device that is placed and moved around the desk to control cursor movements. It has at least two buttons, which may be used to select menu options and to manipulate objects on the screen.

MS-DOS

The most popular version of DOS developed by Microsoft.

Network

A way of connecting computers so that they can share data, software programs as well as hardware such as printers.

Operating system

An operating system consists of a suite of programs that interface between the user, application programs and the processor. It translates commands into the machine language that the computer understands. It also controls the hardware and software. DOS is an example of an operating system.

Options

The third part of a DOS command, which gives optional information to the operating system about how the command is to be executed. Also known as *switches*.

Parameters

The second part of a full DOS command, after the command itself. It tells DOS what to act upon or where to do something. This part of the command is not compulsory for all commands, but it is for some.

Path

This is the route that leads from the root directory on a disk to a particular file. It includes all the intervening directories between the root directory and the file.

Pathname

The full name of a DOS *file* including the *path* to the file. So a pathname would start from the *drive* letter; followed by all *directories* and sub-directories leading to the one holding the file; and then finally ending with the *filename*.

PC

An acronym for *personal computer*. Since IBM introduced the *IBM PC*, the term PC is used to refer to all IBM PCs as well as the clones.

PC-DOS

Another version of DOS. Stands for *Personal Computer - Disk Operating System*. It was developed by Microsoft specifically for the IBM PC. It is similar to MS-DOS in that most application programs designed for MS-DOS can be used with PC-DOS.

Pipe

A DOS command by which you can

direct output from one command to another.

Program

A set of coded instructions for the computer to perform a specific task. There are two types of programs: *system programs* such as operating systems and *application programs* such as wordprocessors and spreadsheets.

Prompt

When your computer is waiting for you to enter a command or information, it will use a prompt to indicate this, e.g. C:\> is a DOS command prompt.

RAM

An acronym for *Random Access Memory*. Storage memory inside the computer that may be written to and updated by the processor. RAM only holds 'live' data, which means that any updates must be saved on a hard or floppy disk before leaving the application or switching off the computer.

ReadMe file

A file associated with a software package, giving details of minor changes in the package and in the installation of it, which is sometimes omitted in the manuals.

ROM

An acronym for *Read Only Memory*. ROM is a microchip with storage memory that cannot be amended. It is used to hold static information for the computer.

Root directory

The main *directory* on any disk. It is created when the disk is formatted. Other directories and sub-directories are optional but the root directory will always be present in a formatted DOS disk. It is identified by the back slash (\).

Save

A DOS command to write a new file or an amended file onto permanent storage such as a hard disk or a floppy disk.

Scrolling

The method by which you move through a list, e.g. of files, which is too long to display on one screen. This is done by clicking on *scroll arrows* or dragging the *scroll box* in the required direction.

Software

Software consists of instructions written to perform specific tasks. e.g. Bookkeeping, personal organiser.

Source disk

The original disk from which the files are to be copied or moved to a *target disk*.

Subdirectory

A *directory* which is subordinate to another directory, it's *parent*.

Target disk

The disk you are copying or moving files to. Also called the *destination disk*.

Text file

A data file saved in text or ASCII format. That is a file with raw data without any formatting.

Upper memory area

The top 384 kilobytes of the basic one megabyte of memory that DOS can access. It is used for system hardware, such as the display adapter. Unused parts of the upper memory are called *upper memory blocks* and can be used to store device drivers and memory-resident programs.

Upward-compatible

A term used in computing to mean that subsequent versions of hardware or software will be compatible to the original one. In DOS, this means that once a command is introduced, it is usually valid for all subsequent versions of DOS, except when it is discontinued.

Virus

A piece of software that is designed to corrupt information on the computer. It is programmed to run automatically, copy itself and spread to other computers via networks, modems or floppies.

Wildcard

Just like the wildcards used in playing cards, DOS wildcards are used in DOS commands to tell DOS to ignore one or more characters. A question mark in a filename, for instance, means ignore the single character where the question mark is. An asterisk wildcard is used to represent one or more characters.

Windows

A *graphical user interface* which uses rectangular areas on your computer screen to display information and to run applications.

Index

Other Books from Computer Step

The PC Novice's Handbook 2nd edition by Harshad Kotecha ISBN 1-874029-04-0, 128 pages £9.95

The PC Novice's Handbook for Upgrading & Maintenance by Roy Bunce ISBN 1-874029-14-8, 160 pages £9.95

The Complete Guide to Sage Sterling & Accounting by Stephen Jay ISBN 1-874029-10-5, 468 pages £19.95

The Complete Guide to Sage Sterling+2 for Windows by Adele Ward ISBN 1-874029-17-2, 248 pages £14.95

WordPerfect: The Joy of Six by Darren Ingram ISBN 1-874029-08-3, 155 pages £11.95

Computers in Schools by Steve Greenwood ISBN 1-874029-05-9, 144 pages £5.95

Computing for the Terrified! by Steve Greenwood ISBN 1-874029-09-1, 151 pages £6.95

"Everything the beginner needs to know to get started is between these covers" - Practical PC

"The book is written in a clear, easy to understand way that makes it simple to read...." - WordPerfect Magazine

"I've been successfully using Sage for ten years and STILL find this book helpful..." - Finance Director, Wyvern Business Library

In easy Steps Series

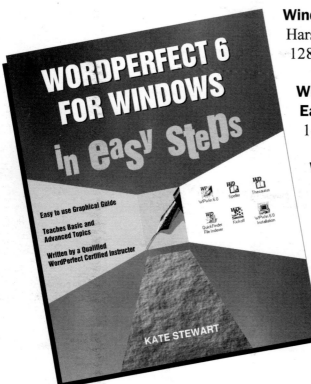

Windows in Easy Steps (v3.1) by Harshad Kotecha ISBN 1-874029-02-4, 128 pages £9.95

Windows for Workgroups 3.11 in Easy Steps by Harshad Kotecha ISBN 1-874029-12-1, 180 pages £14.95

WordPerfect 6 for Windows in Easy Steps by Kate Stewart ISBN 1-874029-11-3, 331 pages £14.95

PageMaker 5 in Easy Steps by Scott Basham ISBN 1-874029-16-4, 220 pages £14.95

Word 6 for Windows in Easy Steps by Scott Basham ISBN 1-874029-16-4, 288 pages £14.95

Excel 5 for Windows in Easy Steps by Roy Roach ISBN 1-874029-15-6, 320 pages £14.95

"a handout on our Introduction to Windows Course....a cost effective solution to providing quality, up to date course material" - Senior Training Manager, NatWest Bank

"....is quite the best book on this subject I have read. The use of concise explanations with copious pictures is the obvious way to learn to use DTP packages and the author uses this technique brilliantly." - The IBM PC User Group

"....one of the best PageMaker 5.0 reference book on the market." - Aldus

"....beautifully clear and simple to follow....Compares favourably with the overpriced American imports." - WordPerfect User Group